ALSO FLEW

GEORGE CHESTERTON

ASPECT DESIGN
Malvern, Worcs. UK

Published by Aspect Design 2008
Malvern, Worcestershire, United Kingdom.

Designed and Printed by Aspect Design
89 Newtown Road, Malvern, Worcs. WR14 1AN
United Kingdom
Tel: 01684 561567
E-mail: books@aspect-design.net
www.aspect-design.net

Cover (image mirrored):
Arnhem, 2·00pm 18th September 1944
by Steven Warwick-Fleming

ISBN 978-1-905795-21-5

ALSO FLEW

GEORGE CHESTERTON

Contents

DEDICATION

*This book is dedicated to all those
who were not able to queue for their demob suits.*

Without the encouragement of my stepdaughter, Tamsin Sridhara, this book would never have seen the light of day. Initially, it took the form of E-mails, which she was helping me to master. She persuaded me to carry on long after I had intended to stop. Indeed, I was originally going to call it, 'Letters to Tamsin'.

Apart from my gratitude to Tamsin, I am indebted to Dr Dennis Williams for the use of his library of pictures, and for permission from Steven Warwick-Fleming and William Dring to reproduce their paintings. I am also grateful to Stanley Collis for his Bowden photographs. Then finally, I very much appreciate the patience and forbearance of everyone at Aspect Design.

*Pastel drawing of George Chesterton
by the Official War Artist William Dring R.A.*

Leaving school

Leaving school, aged 18 in 1941 was an amazing experience. Hitler had overrun most of Europe, the Americans had no intention of joining the war, the battle of the Atlantic was going extremely badly, rationing was beginning to bite, and yet neither I nor any of my friends doubted that we would win the war. Fifty-seven of us left Malvern in July 1941; twenty went into the army, ten into the navy, fourteen into the RAF and three became medical students. The remaining ten are not recorded in any way; I am sure that all of them would have wound up in one of the Services. By volunteering straight away you could choose which service you went into. My father took me straight to Worcester at the end of term, this was the nearest RAF recruiting centre, and I signed on the dotted line. Whether I expected to be whisked off straight away I don't remember, but I was told that I would be called for a preliminary medical in Worcester in about a week. And so it proved…

I had to report to the old Corn Exchange which was manned by a collection of local doctors, some of them retired. It was here I met my first senior NCO, absolutely the salt of the earth. I had no fears about this medical, my last few weeks at school had been given over to endless sport, so I was superbly fit. Imagine my shattering horror when the nice NCO said 'I am sorry young man you have been passed as unfit for aircrew.' Needless to say, tears welled up. I could not believe it. The wonderful NCO said 'Wait here.' He disappeared with all my documents and was only gone ten minutes, he reappeared to tell me that because I had acne on my shoulders I would not be able to wear a parachute harness, but he said, 'I persuaded the senior MO that this was nonsense, so he has passed you fit for aircrew, you will be called for a full aircrew medical in Birmingham within four weeks, and jolly good luck to you.'

SECOND MEDICAL

In exactly a month, I had a letter asking me to report to the medical centre in Birmingham. This was a very different set up to the one in Worcester. I don't remember what the building had been. It was clean and looked very modern and efficient. The staff, that is to say the medical staff, were all young Royal Air Force officers. When I arrived I had to report to one of those excellent senior non-commissioned officers, a Flight Sergeant in this instance. He outlined the programme of the day, and I started on my trek round all the different departments; never have I had so comprehensive a medical examination. I don't remember all the sequence, but of course, there was heart, lungs and eyes; this last was an anxiety to me because my father was colour blind, and I was afraid I might have inherited the same problem. As I went round from one department to another I went into partnership, as it were, with another young man; he was about 25, very strong, fairly uncouth and, it turned out, a coal miner. Coal miners had just been released to apply for air crew and submarine duties. He and I went round all day together, this in itself was an experience for me, especially since it was the first time anyone had called me 'mate'. There were several stages which caused me particular anxiety, for example; a sinister gadget containing mercury, the idea was that you had to blow down a tube and support the column of mercury and hold it there while your blood pressure, and various other tests, were taken. I had, of course, heard about this contraption and was very nervous about it. When the doctor asked me to blow into the tube (which had a very clever mouthpiece designed so that you could not put your tongue in the aperture to hold the mercury up without blowing), I gave all my puff to try to hold the mercury up the column, then, for the first and, I hope, the last time in my life, I woke up on the floor saying, 'Where am I?' The doctor said, 'What on earth are you doing, no one has ever done that before.' I explained that I was very anxious about this test. This delightful man simply said, 'You've really no reason to worry, but I will now have to send you back to the heart and ear specialist, then you must come back here and we will go through this test again. But don't worry about it.' About half an hour later, I was back to have another go. 'Just take it gently, hold the mercury, not as high as you thought you had to, all I am doing is just testing your blood pressure when you are under some stress.' Anyway, I sailed through in the end. He was the last of the doctors and sent me down to administration where the friendly Flight Sergeant told me what would happen next. He told me that I would almost certainly not be called for air crew training for six months, I could either go home and have what was called deferred service, or I could join at once whereon I would probably be given jobs cleaning lavatories and other menial tasks. Obviously, I chose deferred service, and this meant that I would be able to go home and await the call for training. A footnote to this day; my young coalmining friend, muscular and healthy looking though he appeared, was turned down on medical grounds, being told that he would have to have all his teeth out before he could be passed fit for training. He was not the least put out because he had had a day away from the pit on full pay, and he didn't really mind whether he joined the air force or not.

DEFERRED SERVICE

When I heard that I had to take deferred service I was disappointed at first, but, when I got used to the idea, I realised how wonderful it would be to have six months before actually putting on uniform; after all, it must have been nearly twelve years since I had had such a continuous spell at home. As I settled down I realised the war had to go on, so I joined the ATC and the Home Guard, both of which had two evening meetings a week, and the Home Guard had an exercise every other weekend. Also, I felt I had to get some sort of job; my father approached a farmer friend of his, a rather pink, short, fat man, who was known locally – not to his face – as Piggy Bates. He very decently arranged a three-day week for me, and paid me half a crown an hour for three, six hour days. To get to his farm I had to cycle about eight miles, so each of those days was fairly full. I learned a number of modest skills, for example, I learnt to operate a circular saw, to make silage and to cord wood. It was also exciting to actually earn money on my own account.

When I went to the farm I was given tasks on my own, for example, when I made silage I was in the silage pit, while tractor loads of various green vegetation were delivered. I also discovered that the molasses used in making

Down on the farm, January 1942.

14

silage was excellent on a piece of bread. So I was able to add it to the wonderful sandwich lunches which my mother provided. One sunless day, I was miles out from the farm, stacking wood into piles which were known as cords. I had forgotten my watch, there wasn't a house in sight, and I had no means of knowing the time, so after I thought I had done a full morning's work, I had my lunch, then I set to and did a long afternoon stint – so I thought – and then climbed on my bike and set off for home. As I rounded the corner near the vicarage I could see the church clock. I naturally expected to read something like 5·00pm or perhaps later, but no, it was just before two o'clock! Needless to say, I did not go back to do the extra two hours.

The ATC proved to be a useful exercise, because there was quite a lot of preliminary training which stood me in good stead. The officer commanding was a man I enormously respected, he was only about thirty-five, but had just been invalided out of the Royal Air Force, being given six months to live. In fact he died very shortly after I left home, early the next year.

The Home Guard was exactly as portrayed in *Dad's Army*. As probably the youngest and most active member of the Tenbury platoon I was singled out to demonstrate the most effective way of doing the exercises we were given and, in fact, during physical training I had to stand in front so that all the elderly, the farmers and the infirm could follow what, they thought, was a good example. Some of the weekend exercises were really quite amazing, for example, I was put in charge of a section one evening, just after Christmas, there was snow on the ground; I had persuaded the members of the section to come with old sheets so that they could be fully camouflaged. Our task was to make a night attack on a position defended by the rest of the platoon. So successful was our camouflage that they never saw us coming, and we won a victory without, as it were, a shot being fired.

In addition to all this, I took on a paper round with another chap. We had a little trolley and called from house to house collecting newspapers, and then took took them back to a centre where there was an amazing machine, which compressed the papers so they were as hard as a brick, then, presumably, these bricks were taken off to be recycled for further use.

It was, as I had anticipated, wonderful to be at home, my mother coped with rationing and all the difficulties in the most amazing way. I had always admired her, but I particularly did in the way that she never fussed – because she was a highly nervous person – never once did she say, 'be careful with the circular saw', or, 'watch out for that newspaper press', or express anxieties about the ridiculous Home Guard exercises, all things she must have felt, but she never said a word.

Pearl Harbour

While I was at home, momentous things were happening in the war. The battle in the Atlantic was going desperately badly. Hitler's armies were storming through Russia, covering, it seemed, hundreds of miles a day. Although the worst of the Blitz seemed to be over, bombing, particularly on London, was a frequent reality. There were reverses in North Africa. The only bright spot seemed to be the efforts of the Royal Air Force. We know now that the bombing they carried out was almost totally ineffective, but that something offensive was happening was very good for morale.

Then, in December, came Pearl Harbour. This, at least, brought the Americans into the war, although, with typical British arrogance, we didn't think they would be much use. The only time I ever doubted the outcome of the war was the awful day when the *Repulse* and the *Prince of Wales* were sunk off the coast of Malaya. However, I didn't doubt long.

At home, it was lovely, I was given what had been a staff sitting room in wealthier times. There were still a few young people about, so we used to have monopoly parties, which went on for hours. To swell the family coffers, which my father had tapped severely (I suspect quite a lot had gone on the horses) paying guests became the order of the day. A dear old thing, Miss Jackson by name, had come to live with us to escape the London bombing. My father was convinced she had a false bun attached to her hair, I peered and peered, but was never quite sure. We called her Jackie, not to her face of course, but she must have heard because at breakfast one day she said, 'Do please call me Jackie'. She had a vast supply of enormous hats. A flat was provided for the Ludoviccies, a German Jewish couple who spent their lives playing bridge. Apparently, he had a convention named after him.

My father, the vicar, was the most remarkable jack of all trades. Everyone was encouraged to produce as much food as they possibly could, and he set an excellent example. The vicarage had an old pigsty, so we kept pigs; we knew them as Flanagan and Alan. The trouble was, we became so fond of them that, when the day came that poor Flanagan had to go, there was a feeling of deep gloom, and Alan then pined for his brother and began losing weight, so he had to go as well. My father was brilliant, he cured the bacon and ham himself. We also kept chickens and had a non-stop supply of the most wonderful eggs, I have often wondered what he fed them on.

K

K was the love of the first part of my life. She first appeared on the scene when she was brought by my father to watch cricket at Malvern in 1941. I was immediately smitten, but the opposite was certainly not the case. Had she not come again with my father, who was teaching her to drive, we would probably have never met again as she thought the odiously conceited, captain of Malvern's cricket team was to be avoided. With reluctance, she was persuaded to give her address which, at this time, was at a 'finishing school' the other side of Worcester. By the end of term, constant attention, a great many letters and much flattery had begun to win her round. K was persuaded to come and stay at home, and fairly frequent visits followed during my long period of deferred service, to the point where an understanding developed between us. Our courting was gloriously old-fashioned and simple; we talked for hours, we walked, we played tennis, until we began to find we were miserable when we were not in each other's company.

It was K who first put on uniform, but I followed soon after; so, particularly after she was posted to Scotland, our contact was by horribly brief phone calls and enormously long, sentimental letters. We had one short leave together at home, where she was persuaded, against her mother's wishes, that we should get engaged; on the firm understanding that we would not marry until after the war. Then came Canada and a long year's absence. Both of us wrote frequent letters, which were limited in real news and occasionally censored, but filled with endearments which meant much at the time. K was posted to Middle Wallop, not far from Winchester. This was much more interesting for her; as an 'Ops' girl, her time in Scotland had been quiet to the point of boredom. Middle Wallop was a different kettle of fish, the girls worked a three watch system, that meant eight hours on and sixteen off, round-the-clock every day of the week. Leave was scarce; a 48 hour pass came round once a month.

Air Crew Reception Centre

We had as jolly a Christmas as was possible. Then, in February 1942, came the letter which I knew had to come. It was addressed to '1578139 AC2 G.H. Chesterton', giving me joining instructions, seven days away and, of course, enclosing a railway warrant. An AC2 was the lowest form of life in the Royal Air Force, but we were singled out in a modest way by having white flashes in our caps. ACRC, known as 'Arsietarsie' or more accurately, 'Air Crew Reception Centre', was in St John's Wood. The aim, I suppose, was threefold. Firstly, to fit us out with uniform and all the essential extras, then to give us an amazing cocktail of drugs to fight off cholera, typhoid, malaria and, I believe, a host of other complaints. Then, thirdly, to introduce us to military discipline and all that that entailed.

The group I was with was a flight of 29 policemen and me. The police, who were normally reserved, had recently been released for aircrew duties. I shared a room with two of them, Bert and Percy. This was a culture shock of major proportions. Never before, for example, had I met anyone who slept in their underclothes. Bert was something of a bully, but Percy was a dear. I suppose they were both about 25. In charge of our flight was the odious Corporal Jones, he had the difficult task of teaching us the ways of the service and, amongst other things, he introduced us to 'biscuits'; so named because the mattresses, which they made up in three pieces, looked like enormous dog biscuits. We were issued with blankets and sheets, how we made our beds was immaterial. It was the stacking of the biscuits, the folding of the blankets and the laying out of our kit, that concerned Corporal Jones, and it had to be just right. It was somewhat galling that the quarters in which we lived, really a collection of apartments, had been awarded some important architectural prize in 1937. We didn't live in actual squalor, but the rooms were devoid of furniture apart from a small locker for each occupant, the floor boards on which we slept were bare and there were basic black-out curtains on the windows, nothing else. Washing facilities were totally inadequate for the numbers involved.

The handing out of kit was a tedious routine, but efficient just the same. Corporal Jones sidled up later to offer a few shillings for the odd shirt, which, he said, we wouldn't need. We heard on the grapevine that a month or two later, he was found out, court martialled and reduced to the ranks.

There was no problem for Corporal Jones over teaching our flight to march, or learn elementary drill, we had all done it before. He knew of every coffee shop down the back streets of St John's Wood, and that's where we spent a lot of our time.

Our meals were taken in the London Zoo restaurant, which had been taken over. The zoo was still open to the public, although for obvious reasons, the dangerous animals had been removed to Whipsnade. A knife, fork and spoon were issued to everyone and were carried to all meals; they were known as 'irons'. After each meal one's irons had to be washed in disgusting buckets which became greasy, and the water cold.

One day, one of the WAAFS serving out food, accidentally bounced two potatoes on the floor, picked them up, and put them on my plate. The Orderly Officer made a routine visit, the duty Sergeant calling out, 'Orderly Officer, any complaints?' I was sitting with Bert, he egged me on to complain, which I did. 'I can see nothing wrong with those potatoes. Sergeant, take this airman's name.' said the Orderly Officer. Next day, I had two hours peeling potatoes!

Jabs at ACRC

The medical centre at ACRC was in a vast Georgian building. For some reason, the chilly basement area was set aside for the jabs we had been promised. It was February, and quite cold enough. Doctors, nurses and orderlies gave jabs to the long queues of airmen that stretched along a winding basement corridor; each victim shuffled forward, stripped to the waist, so that both arms were exposed. The needles were plunged in from either side, there was no question of frequent new needles. They were used until they were too blunt to penetrate the skin, or so we believed. As we left the building, we were told that we had twenty-four hours off-duty. I felt fine, so climbed on a bus to go down Baker Street, but I began to weaken, and went into the first cinema I came to, *Dumbo* was the film. Two hours later, I could hardly move either arm, and walked to the bus stop with difficulty. I literally fell off the bus; some old dear thought I was drunk. How I managed to walk the last few hundred yards I shall never know. Bert and Percy were spark out, I fumbled down my biscuits, fell on them, dragging over a blanket, and came to some twelve hours later.

My next posting came through, I was to move to 'No. 4, Initial Training Wing' at Paignton. All my policeman friends were going elsewhere. On our last day, the flight was marched by Corporal Jones round to Lord's Cricket Ground, part of which had been taken over by the air force. We were marched into the Long Room, devoid of furniture, with bare boards and, of course, not a picture to be seen. The actual ground was covered with coils of barbed wire, and a barrage balloon was anchored on the nursery ground. We were there for an 'FFI'. I had no idea what that was. 'Down trousers,' said Jones, and then a medical orderly came round, with a spatular like object and inspected each one of us. I learned that 'FFI' stood for 'Free From Infection'!

The next day, I caught the train to Paignton, with few regrets.

Barrage balloon at Lord's nursery ground.

Initial Training Wing Paignton

Paignton was a joyous contrast. It was like going back to school; a regular routine, and lots of games. It was imaginative of the powers that be to have decided to put together a flight all of whom had come through the Air Training Corps.

ITWs were strung round the coast in large resorts where there were hotels, which could be adapted for cadets. Torquay had two ITWs, Newquay, Scarborough, Weston-super-Mare and Paignton each had one. We were based in the Hydro Hotel, at the right-hand end of the Esplanade, looking out to sea. There must have been at least 10 acres of open grassland before the beach. In common with piers all round the coast, a fifty foot slice had been taken out of Paignton pier, and the beach – which was out of bounds – was covered with coils of barbed wire. During my first week, three idiots decided to swim round the pier; it was quite cold and also choppy, one of them got into difficulty and, despite frantic efforts to reach him, he drowned. My first experience of a casualty.

The routine was one of lectures, navigation, principles of flight, engines, meteorology, lots of PT and drill. We were encouraged to take responsibility, and I made sure I did. There was a very smart chap called Metz, whom I confess I didn't like. He always held the top slot in the cadet hierarchy; however hard I tried to push him off.

Our squadron commander was a superlative man, the officer in charge of our flight was an efficient, officious, former bank clerk. He used to try and catch us out. For example, if we had to do guard duty, he would try and sneak up on you and, when challenged, although we knew it was him, if you didn't say, 'Advance friend and be recognised', you were in for a rocket. For all his faults he was fair, even though he demanded officiously high standards. Discipline was tight and one incident I remember well; our respected squadron commander had summoned the whole unit and we feared the worst. He said, 'I have a particularly serious and disgusting matter to report; a used French letter was found this morning on the steps of the hotel. Such disgraceful behaviour will not be tolerated.' I was shocked to the core, but was so naive that I had to have the enormity of the offence explained to me.

No. 4 ITW. GHC is in the back row on the extreme left.

I shared a room with three chaps of my own age, Jack from Essex, David from Yorkshire, and Andrew from London. We all got on well. They could not believe that anyone could be as unworldly wise as I was; for example, I had never been into a pub. They set about my education. They even bribed the daughter of the landlord of the Harbour Inn, who rejoiced in the wonderful name Diana le Roy Thompson, to kiss me at the end of an evening which we had all spent together. I was horrified. I did, however, like her, and I took her out a few times. We even won a waltz competition at a local hop, and I once took her to the local theatre where we saw a crummy play called *The Dominant Sex*. But I made sure she never kissed me again.

Our room in the Hydro was on the ground floor and overlooked the local municipal laundry, my roommates made friends with the girls who worked there; we had the smartest and cleanest clothes, particularly collars, in the whole squadron. Roughly opposite there was the flat of an attractive and bosomy young woman, who made sure, each morning, that as many cadets as possible saw her dressing. I tried not to look.

The services often have elephant-like memories. While I was at Paignton, the medical side caught up with my acne problem, which so nearly stopped my flying career before it started. I was summoned to the medics; an extremely nice MO said that I was to have a four-week course of jabs, only one a week, but in my backside. The second week, the doctor inquired whether I would mind a trainee WAAF nurse doing the injection. After two or three pathetic little pricks, he said, 'Come on plunge the needle in', she did! The following week I displayed the most wonderful multicoloured bruise, the doctor laughed and said, 'Don't worry, that girl has decided to be a cook.'

Visual Morse was an essential part of our course at Paignton. Light signals were flashed with an Aldis lamp to about a hundred cadets scattered in pairs, on the grass area near the beach. One of each pair reading and the other writing down the signals. One morning, Jack, who was scribing for me called out, 'There are three

"Spits" coming in fast. My God, they're not Spitfires; they've got black crosses.' They were FW190s. Two peeled off for Torquay, and one for Brixham. The bombs they dropped did considerable damage, particularly in Torquay where 20 cadets were killed.

Near the end of our twelve week stay in Paignton I had persuaded my future mother-in-law that K and I should publish our engagement. The Squadron Commander ushered me into his office and warmly congratulated me on the announcement of my engagement and then gently but firmly reminded me that I was RAF *Volunteer Reserve* and not, as the announcement had said, a *regular* member of the Royal Air Force.

Towards the end of our course I played the odd game of cricket in Torquay for training command, using boots borrowed from the squadron commander. To my great shame, I discovered – months later – that I had never returned them. A selected few were held back after the course, to our great disgust, to practise a drill display for the King, who was due to visit Paignton a fortnight later. I remember being shocked at how made up he appeared. The pity was that many of my immediate friends had been posted on; for example, I never saw Jack or Andrew again. The course was now complete, and I was sent on ten days embarkation leave.

ATLANTIC CROSSING

A number of the Paignton crowd foregathered at Heaton Park near Manchester, a holding station, some unfortunates spent weeks at this grim spot, but we were there a mere twenty-four hours, before chugging north on a troop train to Gourock. Strictly forbidden, I managed to smuggle a postcard home via a railwayman, it simply said, 'On our way.'

As we unloaded from the train, humping our kit bags, we were taken out to an American transport at dusk, which must have been near midnight, since it was midsummer. We scrambled aboard from the tender and assembled in an enormous common area. Bed space was allotted in the holds, these had been converted to make this 14,000 ton transport a troopship. On the recent west-east crossing she had made, there had been 3,000 GIs aboard, each bunk had been shared by three men in rotation. There were only about 600 of us, so we each had our own bunk; under the pillow of mine was a copy of *The Mill on the Floss*, I still have it, and have often wondered about its original owner. The convoy, which consisted of three transports escorted by a US battleship – the *New York*, a veteran of 1918 – and four destroyers, slipped quietly down the Clyde at first light.

The speed of the convoy was dictated by the elderly battleship, about fourteen knots. There was a heavy swell running as we left the protection of the Clyde estuary. In no time, I retired to my bunk and for the next twenty-four hours would have welcomed a torpedo. I slowly developed sea-legs, of a sort, and crawled up on deck to find a quiet spot where movement seemed less obvious. After three days I was well enough to take up the chores we were all allotted. It was my misfortune to be given cook-house duties. The galley was an enormous, American-style canteen, the actual mess area seated at least 200, and the kitchens smelt like a chocolate factory. My first task was to scour out the porridge vat; the only way to tackle it was to stand inside it, this rapidly reduced me to the state I was in on day one. A sympathetic sergeant gave me time off, and then put me onto wiping tables.

It is now known that convoys were routed to avoid U-boats (thanks to *Enigma),* we went hundreds of miles north, well inside the Arctic Circle. On about day six, a large ship's lifeboat came into view; it proved to be empty. The four escorting destroyers steamed past it in line astern for some target practice; not a hit was achieved and, somewhat self-consciously, one of the destroyers sank it by ramming.

During the last few days of our crossing, we were given a series of talks on how to behave in Canada, mostly the advice was obvious, but I do particularly remember that something you do not do is to ask a girl to have 'a quick knock-up' before playing tennis.

After 12 days at sea we sailed quietly into New York harbour, enjoying the view of the Statue of Liberty, something that I never dreamt I would see.

MONCTON, NEW BRUNSWICK, CANADA.

So in June we arrived in Moncton having travelled up by train from New York.

I was not so lucky this time, this was a holding station, and for two months a lot of us were held there. Most wartime friendships are understandably transitory. I had, to date, been on friendly terms with nearly everyone, but at Moncton I met Ted Howard; he came from the same sort of background, we had much in common and became real friends. We had much free time, so we explored our part of New Brunswick. The port of St. John's, which has, I believe, the highest rise and fall of tide in the world, offered us the spectacle of reversing falls, and the locals were proud of 'magnetic hill', which was an interesting and spectacular optical illusion. Take a car apparently to the bottom of the hill, let off the brakes, and it quietly freewheels 'up' the hill. Ted and I explored these

First Cricket Match, July 1942, Australia v. England.
GHC is in the back row 4th from right.

Above: Moncton.

Right: Magnetic Hill,
near Moncton.

and many other places of interest. He had the most amazing and old-fashioned swimming costume, which to the astonishment of the locals he brought into use once or twice, when we went to a neighbouring beach.

There were hundreds of cadets of all nationalities in Moncton, including many Australians. A number of us decided to arrange a Test match. No-one had, I suspect, ever played cricket in New Brunswick before, so it was not easy. The Sports Department had all the essentials of kit and, with much hard work, we prepared a ground. It had, of course, to be a matting wicket and, clumsy though it was, we had no choice but to play in our battle dress. The sad thing to report is that the Australians won the match.

I suppose we appreciated the fact that there was no food rationing, nor, of course, any blackout, but it was a frustrating period and when, at last, a posting to Alberta came, it was a great relief.

ACROSS CANADA

It was extraordinary that Ted Howard, who had very poor eyesight, was able to pass his aircrew medical. He claimed that the doctors concerned did not pick up the fact that he was wearing contact lenses. Contact lenses were in a very early stage of development, and Ted must have been one of the first to use them. The lenses were bulky and quite difficult to fit – they covered the whole eye, but he was convinced that at his medical they did not spot the fact that he was wearing lenses until nearly the end, and felt that they decided to use him as a guinea pig, and see if it was possible to go through aircrew training using the lenses.

We left Moncton with few regrets and set off on the amazing train journey across Canada, a distance which was greater than we had already travelled from home. The train we travelled in was of great age, it had very solidly-built coaches that contained few modern conveniences; there were solid bunks, reasonable seats and, at the end of each coach, there was a common area, rather similar to those seen in old western films – in the middle was a copper spitoon. We had a longish break in Montréal, and most of us took the opportunity of exploring the city like tourists. The journey on was spectacular, but became extremely monotonous, there were literally hundreds of miles of lakes and forest. So we had to while away the time. One of our group was a keen bridge player, and set about teaching some of us lesser mortals. Bridge is, in a way, rather like riding a bicycle; once you have learnt the basics, this knowledge stays with you for life. Needless to say, it does not

Ted Howard

necessarily make you a *good* bridge player, but I was glad that I took the trouble to learn on this journey. I think it lasted four days and nights, the catering was done by civilians, and so was much more than adequate. The train disgorged numbers of cadets at various destinations, because there were so many training bases in, what was called, the Empire training scheme. We stopped at places with lovely names like Medicine Hat and Assiniboyne. We carried on to the far West leaving the provinces of Manitoba and Saskatchewan behind as we headed into Alberta. We changed trains at Calgary and set off north on the relatively short three hour journey to Innisfail.

Montréal

Bowden, Alberta

On the RAF transport that carried us from Innisfail station there were a number of embryo pilots, with at least two weeks experience. Typically, they were real prophets of gloom, 'The Stearman was a very difficult aircraft to fly', 'It was very easy to ground loop – two ground loops and you were scrubbed'. Bowden was interesting in that all the ground subjects were taught by civilians, and because there was such a major non-service element the station closed at weekends – unless the course fell well behind schedule. Members of Course 61 foregathered the next morning, most of us had travelled across Canada together, but there were several new faces; three young army officers who were transferring to the RAF, and several senior NCOs from various ground branches. We were quartered in large spacious buildings, modern and purpose-built, rather strangely, we slept in two tier bunks. David Bethell, who was a former police inspector, and a product of Hendon Police College, was 31 and at the top age limit for training; he was above me, and in the next bunk was my particular Moncton friend, Ted Howard, and above him was David Brooks. For the first week, we were totally committed to ground subjects. Ted and I made

Stearman and Tigers.

the most of the first weekend, hitch hiking our way to Banff in the Rockies. The Canadians were quite astonishingly generous in giving lifts, often for hundreds of miles, and it was not untypical for a driver to go tens of miles out of his way. Banff was all it was cracked up to be and Ted was, as usual, great company.

At the end of our second week, flying started; the routine was simple, flying one morning, with ground subjects in the afternoon, and then the procedure was reversed next day. The great moment arrived when we were introduced to the Stearman; this was a real aeroplane, and there were rows of them, a few Tiger Moths were on the end of the line, these were used for instrument flying. I was introduced to my instructor, Warrant Officer Stevens, a wonderful pilot with two years instructing under his belt. He was fed up and longed to get to England on operations. (He soon had his wish; he was converted on to Mosquitoes and was sadly killed on his second sortie.) He greeted me in a fairly unfriendly manner and told me which aircraft to climb into. He offered few preliminary remarks before he started up the aircraft and said, 'Your first flight is for familiarisation and I will do most of the flying.' He took off without so much as a friendly word, and climbed away at maximum revs, he pointed out a few landmarks as he threw the Stearman about the sky. 'I will now show you a stall and a spin or two.' He pulled the stick hard back until we flipped sickeningly into a spin, he recovered from that, and almost immediately threw us into another. I was feeling sick and frightened. 'Now we will do another and you can recover, remember stick forward and opposite rudder.' We started spinning to the left. 'Now recover,' he said, 'Don't bind on the stick, boy. Alright, I have it. We will now try a few simple turns; you have control. Don't bind on the stick! Don't bind on the stick! Alright I'll take her back.' He did a few aerobatics and some low flying. I closed my eyes and prayed that it would end soon. At last, when we climbed out, he said, 'You won't see me again, I go on leave tomorrow.' As I returned, miserably, to the students crew room, I overheard him talking to a new young Sergeant instructor, 'You are taking on young Chesterton tomorrow; don't waste too much time on him, he is a total washout.' If nothing else had done, *this* stirred my determination; but Sergeant Tarry was a very different kettle of fish. He was courteous and patient, very positive and determined that his first pupil should succeed.

Bowden

David Bethell was as shattered by his first flying experience as I had been, in many ways more so, because it took so long for him to get over the prospect of flying with anything but dread. He used to sit in the crew room, trembling, as the hatch, which communicated with the instructors room, came back, 'Bethell get into 216', he would leap to his feet as though he was going to execution. Very sensibly the chief instructor insisted that they should persevere with him; it was twelve hours before he went solo.

The initial agony that both David and I suffered was accentuated by Ted Howards' reaction to his first flights; he was overjoyed and excited. 'Wasn't that marvellous,' he said when he first came down, and quickly clammed up when he saw how miserable David and I were. Nonetheless for the first week of flying he was unable to hide his joy and excitement. Then very slowly, and sadly, this began to turn to disappointment. It will be remembered that there was the astonishing experiment of allowing him to fly with contact lenses, this was, unfortunately, proving a failure, despite endless efforts, he could not judge height near the ground; he nearly always levelled out about eight feet too high. His instructor, and the delightful chief flying instructor, persevered beyond the normal limits, but, in the end, he had to be failed. Failed pilots were sent to Trenton in Ontario, where they were usually remustered as navigators. Ted's departure was a great blow to me, we had become close friends, but, typical of wartime friendships, we swore to write on a regular basis. I have not heard from him since. (Very much later I heard that he became an Intelligence Officer in the Service. After the war he became Lord Mayor of London following in the footsteps of his father.) David was a very great help to me in the ground school, where I found navigation a considerable test. Each morning, I was woken by a

Ted Howard, BANFF, August 1942.

rustle of paper in the bunk above me, the click of a lighter, and then the apparently blissful first taste of tobacco for the day, this clearly ecstatic experience put me on the road to smoking, and I didn't look back over the next thirty years.

The weather was perfect, and it is difficult to imagine conditions that could be better for learning to fly. The air was clear and visibility endless, it was nearly impossible to get lost, although one or two did. The Rockies rose up in the West, there was a north-south railway line, and at each station on this route there were enormous grain elevators, with the name of the place clearly painted on the roof, and readable for several miles.

After the early horrors I began to enjoy myself, Sergeant Tarry was a perfect instructor, patient, thorough and meticulous. He paid more attention to airmanship than I am sure did most instructors; airmanship could be compared to road safety instruction by a driving tutor. Look before every turn and scan the sky

Grain elevators

before any violent manoeuvre. Circuits and bumps occupied early flying lessons, then quite out of the blue, Tarry tapped me on the shoulder, undid his harness and climbed out, 'Okay, you're on your own, do one easy circuit and come in.' There is no experience in the world like the first solo. I taxied out gently, carefully did all my cockpit drills, turned onto the runway, eased the throttle steadily forward, a little touch of the rudder to keep her straight,

Stearmans and Tigers

watch the speed, 50, 60, 70. Ease back on the stick and lift off; climbing at full revs to 500 feet, ease back a bit on the throttle; at 800 feet start a gentle, climbing turn to the left until, at 1,000 feet, the runway is at right angles. Throttle back and level out, turning through 90° to have the port wing running, as it were, along the runway. Do all the cockpit checks for landing; brakes off, mixture rich, fuel level okay, and then turn another 90° – looking carefully first, of course – ease the throttle back to let down to 800 feet; look left and turn to line up on the runway, a little less throttle, keep the nose up – but watch the speed, less throttle and descend steadily to cross the fence about 10 feet up; close the throttle and then come back slowly on the stick to finish 10 yards down the runway, on all three wheels, in a perfect three-point landing. Marvellous!

From then on the solo time increased daily. Circuits and bumps dominated, particularly at Netook, the satellite grass airfield. Stearmans were buzzing in and out, round and round, like so many hornets. Little gophers popped their heads up, often in the middle of a take off run, but I never saw one hit. Round and round, up and down, doing the checks ad nauseam, and then sadly disaster struck. 'The Professor', as we called him, (a small, studious and delightful man, like David Bethell at the upper age limit, with greying hair, and later destined to be an instructor) struck the Stearman of David Brooks, his propeller slicing through the instructor's empty cockpit, almost cutting the aircraft in half. This was at about 800 feet. David had little chance, although he must have reacted very quickly; for he managed to get out of the cockpit and pull the ripcord of his parachute, but, sadly, he was just too low. The Professor managed to land his damaged aircraft, and no blame was attached to him, it was all put down to inexperience. The accident cast a gloom over the whole station. I was one of the rifle party, eight of us. We were drilled and instructed by an RAF police corporal, as were the bearer party. A few days later, the full military funeral took place in Innisfail churchyard. I remember being touched and impressed as the sad little cortege drove slowly down the main street and, one after another, locals doffed their hats. There was one wreath on the flag draped coffin, heart rendingly inscribed 'from Mum and Dad'. Our part was passable, with three volleys echoing into the sky, and equally moving was the Last Post – although rather indifferently played. David's grave was alongside three other quite recent ones, all with fresh flowers.

Back to flying; circuits and bumps, forced landing practices, low-flying, steep turns; great fun. With steep turns, the trick was to try and catch your own slipstream. Stalls and recovery from spins had to be underlined in red in the logbook entry. After 25 hours there was the Chief Flying Instructor's check. The CFI had been the private pilot to an Indian maharaja; he was a beautiful pilot and a very nice man. The procedure for the test was standard, take-off and climb away to 5,000 feet, spins to the right and left with recovery, medium and steep turns. Then he would close the throttle and say, 'Please take me back to the airfield and do a glide approach and landing.' The day for my test came; his office was in the control tower; I was detailed to wait for him. I hung my helmet on a convenient peg and waited nervously, until he was ready. 'Okay Chesterton, lets go,' he said. I grabbed the nearest helmet and it turned out to be, horror of horrors, David's – from 10 days before – still matted with not-wholly-congealed blood. The CFI saw what had happened and, with abject apologies, ran back to fetch my helmet – not an auspicious start. However, all went well with the test, the steep turns were perfect, and then came the usual routine of the closed throttle. I located the airfield, did all my checks, joined the circuit for a glide approach and landing, all went smoothly until the final leg. I knew I was 200 feet too high. Biggles then came to my rescue; I remembered how he had let quickly down into a small field by side slipping. So, in desperation, I followed his example: 'Full right rudder, stick hard over to the left, keep the nose up, but watch the speed'; we went down as if in a lift; over the fence, now centralise everything, ease back on the stick. The landing was so gentle that it wouldn't have broken the skin of a rice pudding. We taxied in and the CFI said, 'Well done, but I would rather you stuck to more normal glide approach and landings.'

With the CFI's test over there seemed to be less need for anxiety, but there were several important hurdles still to be negotiated, notably instrument flying, night flying, cross country, and aerobatics. Instrument flying took place in Tiger Moths, and this meant not only grasping the important principle of total

Stan Colley and Paul Tarry.

F/O Dew CFI and Stan Colley.

Bowden.

reliance on instruments, but also coping with an aircraft very sensitive on the controls. The instructor would take off with his pupil enveloped by a dark hood; the instruments were familiar, since hours had already been spent on a Link trainer. It was a vitally important stage, two members of the course failed to come to terms with instrument flying and were washed out. Instrument flying led naturally on to night flying, not as alarming as it sounds in the beautiful clear skies of Alberta. That, in its turn, led to cross country flights. As I have suggested earlier, navigation could not be made easier; with two east–west railways and one north–south and, of course, there was always the long line of the Rockies to the west. One of the army sergeants on the course got himself hopelessly lost, making a forced landing over 150 miles away. He was RTU, (returned to unit). There was one other departure from the course, Andrew Wickets, a small chap with a rather moth eaten sandy moustache, who disappeared one morning. 'Andrew's got a dose,' we were told. I had no idea what that meant, and waited to ask David Bethell. 'Oh, he's got VD; he will return in about six weeks when he's cured.' I never saw Andrew again.

When I was at my prep. school there was an officious gym instructor, who loved making us do all sorts of exercises upside down. For example, there was a ladder bridge about twenty feet above the floor, and we had to cross this, upside down, each morning. I hated it, and blame him for my dislike of most aerobatics. Loops and stall terms were fine, but I particularly disliked slow rolls; the object of these was to roll the aircraft completely through 360° without losing height or direction. All the mud and dust from the floor fell into the pilot's face; I never achieved a really decent roll.

The end of the course was approaching, so much in six weeks! The time had come for assessments. In the RAF there were standard assessments; 'Excellent', 'Above Average', 'Average' and 'Below Average'. John Snow – a delightful, scruffy, ill-disciplined character – was a wonderful natural pilot; he went solo after only two hours, and was the only pilot that I knew who was classified 'Excellent'. He went on to be a fighter pilot. I met Snowy, two years later, on the Underground, looking like nothing on earth, but wearing the ribbon of the DFM. He was still a Sergeant, but I could see from his scruffy uniform that there had been crowns sewn on. He saw me looking at this, and said, 'I have been made up to Flight Sergeant twice, the second time I hit some idiot officer, and I was only saved by this,' as he tapped his medal ribbon. 'I am soon going back on OPs,' he said. I never saw him again.

David Bethell had the rare distinction of being passed with a below average assessment; he was too good to lose, and so we moved on to a Royal Air Force station, only some twenty-five miles north, called RAF Penhold.

PENHOLD, ALBERTA

Penhold was only twenty-five miles north of Bowden, near to the little town of Red Deer. Red Deer was very similar to the little town of Innisfail, only rather

David Bethell, Penhold, Dec.1942.

No. 36, Service Flying Training School. GHC 3rd row, far left.

PLAYER'S CIGARETTES

AIRSPEED "OXFORD" ADVANCED TRAINING AIRCRAFT

larger, it still consisted of one main street, but in this there were two Chinese restaurants, one Indian restaurant and two steak bars, one of which was open all night. Imagine the contrast to somebody who came from a small Worcestershire town, slightly larger than Red Deer, but where there was one hotel, which stopped serving food at 7·30 in the evening.

The Royal Air Force station at Penhold was very different from Bowden; it was a genuine Royal Air Force establishment. There was therefore much more evidence of military discipline, there was a physical training programme and all the other things one associates with an established air force base. In many ways this suited me very well, and I was able to get involved in games and sport again; the summer was more or less over, and so I was introduced to basketball. There was a station team, which used to travel around playing matches, mostly against schools. It was a game I immediately took to, and at least two evenings a week were given over to it.

It is worth remembering that in Western Canada, we were enjoying a total freedom from rationing and, of course, from tedious things like blackout; a wonderful contrast to the situation we had left behind in England.

It was only a few days after we left Bowden that we settled into the new training programme. As usual, there were the prophets of gloom; airmen who had joined the course ahead of us a week or two before, and warned us how difficult the Oxford was to fly, how it swung viciously on take off, how the engines cut-out on landing, and how any failure would lead to immediate dismissal from the course. As usual, this was rubbish. The Airspeed Oxford was probably the best of the twin engine training aircraft used by the Royal Air Force, the two other types were the Avro Anson and the Canadian Cessna. The Oxford certainly seemed a vastly advanced aeroplane after the Stearman, partly and obviously because it had two engines, the sophistication of flaps and a retractable undercarriage, not to mention much more advanced instruments and engine controls.

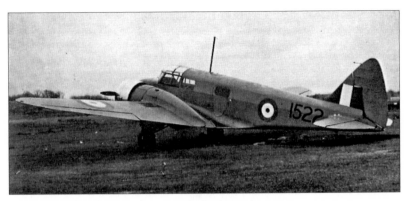

Oxford.

My instructor was an experienced pilot, who had been instructing for two years, he was Warrant Officer Tweed. In the Oxford, the pilot and pupil sat side-by-side, the pupil in the left-hand seat, so it was possible to talk perfectly normally to each other, and this made instruction very much easier. My instructor was a quiet, rather studious man, so I decided on a programme of interesting conversation. Each day I would prepare a topic, I had discovered he was interested in farming, so we would get onto the subject of sheep, ploughing or milking, or other topics I thought might be of interest to him. David Bethell had devised a cunning plan whereby we would sneak into the instructors' office at night so we could read the progress reports on our flying. The report that Tweed wrote on my progress read as follows, 'Flying okay, but he talks too much.' I immediately learnt my lesson, stopped preparing my conversations and stuck to concentrating on my flying and, of course, I got on very much better as a result. David still had problems with his flying, but he also had a very good instructor, who slowly gained David's confidence, and his flying improved as a result.

The Canadians had a wonderful scheme for hospitality and David and I cashed in on this, and made friends in Edmonton and Calgary. The family we came to know in Edmonton were second generation Canadians who ran a small chocolate factory, I suppose we stayed with them about three times. In Calgary, we linked up with some lovely people called Dingle and we spent many weekends with them. We hitch-hiked our way south to stay with them. Colonel Dingle was a lawyer who had returned to the army legal department, based somewhere in Ontario, but he came home most weekends. They were exceptionally kind to both of us.

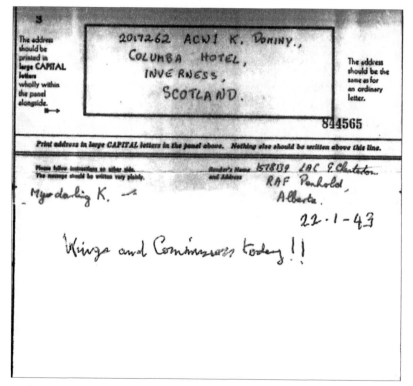

This is an example of the microfilm letter, which was then much in use.

Life was beginning to be rather more serious, not that Bowden had been a holiday camp, but we all began to realise that we were actually preparing to go to war. Our ground exams became more pressing and, for those who were ambitious, there was the aim of going for a Commission; on average the top third of each course received a Commission, the remainder became Sergeant pilots. Apart from personal ambition I was keen to be commissioned for my mother's sake. I now realise she couldn't have cared a fig; my safety was all that concerned her.

We moved to Penhold in September to enjoy a glorious but fairly short autumn. The first snows fell soon after we arrived, but didn't last long, twice we enjoyed the benefits of a Chinook wind – this was known as the snow eater. It was easy to predict the arrival of a Chinook, a long band of cloud preceded it as it swept in from the Rockies. It was only a gentle wind but very warm and dry. About this time, we were issued with 'Caps, Yukon, blue, airmen, for the use of.' This headgear had flaps which dropped down to cover the ears. What an unnecessary piece of equipment, we thought. We realised within a month that they were essential. By mid-November the temperatures

No. 36 Service Flying Training School
Royal Air Force, Penhold

Christmas Dinner 1942
Airmen's Mess

MENU

Cream of Tomato Soup
Roast Turkey   Roast Pork
Roast Potatoes   Creamed Potatoes
Brussels Sprouts   Green Peas
Sage and Onion Stuffing
Cranberry Sauce   Apple Sauce
Rich Brown Gravy
Dinner Rolls

Christmas Pudding
Custard Sauce   Brandy Sauce

Trifle
Cheese   Biscuits   Mince Pies
Apples   Oranges   Grapes   Nuts
Cigarettes   Beer   Minerals

were below freezing and snow was part of the scenery. I began to realise what was to come, when, one morning, the water in the bottom of my newly washed mug froze solid in the hundred yard walk back to the hut. There was one more Chinook in November, but, after that, we lived in a snowscape. The runways were regularly rolled, and they were defined by little Christmas tree-like saplings, surprisingly, they were not very slippery. The temperatures dropped week by week, and we went about our daily routine well muffled up. The aircraft were kept in heated hangers, and started up immediately they were pushed out, otherwise the oil would have frozen. The radial engines were almost totally masked, only a small square aperture was left clear for engine cooling. One week we were beset by blizzards and even colder temperatures; only our sleeping quarters and the dining area were kept open. In fact, to all intents and purposes, the camp closed down, and existed for survival only.

Sgt. for a day, 22nd January 1943.   David Bethell, Wings Day, 1943.

Flying was becoming more advanced, we even landed at other airfields, and there was a great emphasis on instrument flying. The Royal Air Force had a very imaginative scheme whereby there was something called the Standard Flying Panel. The same standard six instruments were fitted to all aircraft – of course, there were many other gauges and dials – but the standard flying instruments were always the same in every aircraft in the Service, and in the same place.

Weekend passes continued to come round regularly, David and I usually hitch-hiked to Calgary, until the weather made hitch-hiking rather a hazard. We used to stay with the Dingles, who were always quite staggeringly hospitable. Later on we took to the train. Coming back one Sunday night the train was held up and nearly everyone climbed out to see what was afoot, the engine had hit a poor horse which had then frozen solid to the front of the train. It had to be hacked away with axes.

On the flying side there was an endless round of cross countries, night flying, bombing practices, and even formation flying. It was clear that the end of the course was in sight. Exams were over; I was passed 'above-average' as a pilot, but my navigation 'needed watching'. Then came the final results, I passed seventh, the first eleven were awarded Commissions. The first three were posted on to an instructors' school; the next three went to coastal command training (David was one of these); and the next three were posted to an Operational Training Unit in Canada, this included me, and was a desperate disappointment – I wanted to come home.

The Wings Parade wound up our stay in Penhold. One by one, we were called forward from where we paraded in a heated hanger, to have our wings pinned on by the Group Captain; a moment of unimaginable pride and excitement. Of the modest achievements in my life, this was the one which gave me the greatest thrill and satisfaction, and I still look back on it with amazement and, I have to say, some pride.

New York

David and I had three weeks to go before starting the next stage of our training; sadly then going our separate ways, but both on the east coast. So we decided to spend part of our leave together in New York. Our meagre pay gave little opportunity for extravagance, although we had not reckoned on the generosity of New Yorkers.

Our journey east across Canada was on a warrant, which included meals, compared to the outward journey some eight months earlier, this was luxury. The train was not just for troops, it was available to the general public as well. The only blot, as far as I was concerned, was a screaming child in the next berth to mine. After three and a half days, David and I arrived in Montréal. The plan was to spend a day there, finding time to visit a tailor to be measured for uniform.

Twenty-four hours later, we set off for New York. The YMCA near Grand Central Station had been recommended to us for use as a base. The quality of the accommodation was amazing, we paid seventy-five cents a day, which included breakfast and all reasonable comforts. On the evening of our arrival there was a fairly heavy snowfall, we imagined this would limit our activities, but, by the next morning, most of it had been cleared! We had the best of all possible worlds; on our greatcoats, which naturally we had to wear most of the time, we wore white flashes on the epaulettes which signified that we were officers, and on our ordinary tunics we had sergeant's stripes and, of course, the glory of our glowing new wings. We were, therefore, in a position to enjoy the quite astonishingly generous hospitality of our hosts, both in what they offered to officers and to other ranks. Although the Battle of Britain had been about two and a half years before, anyone in Royal Air Force uniform was treated with embarrassing adulation. David and I first visited the 'other ranks' entertainment centre. The offers extended were mind-boggling, indeed it was almost impossible to pay for anything. We immediately accepted free tickets to theatres and Radio City Music Hall, but perhaps the most fascinating was an invitation to the Stage Door Canteen. Every night film stars and actresses turned out to dance with, and entertain, the troops; this was enormously popular. Most of the girls were more or less nameless starlets and whilst watching proceedings, somewhat gauchly, I was swept onto the floor by Katharine Hepburn, whose opening query was, 'What does *VR* on your uniform signify?'

'Volunteer Reserve', I told her, 'Oh, how disappointing, I thought it must be *Very Romantic*.' I suppose I had ten minutes dancing with her when she handed me over to Gypsy Rose Lee – probably the best known striptease artiste ever; she was charming and swept me round the floor at a breathtaking pace. We went to the Rockefeller Centre for an ice show, to the Fulton Theatre to see

Arsenic and Old Lace, to the Henry Miller's theatre to see *Jamie,* and to Radio City Music Hall. Through the Officer's Club I was introduced to a charming elderly lady, who wore diamonds the size of pigeon's eggs; she arranged for me to take her eighteen year-old granddaughter, Gwen McKonky, to the Wedgwood Room of the Waldorf Astoria. We got on like a house on fire, and I had to keep reminding myself that I was already engaged.

By day, David and I went up the Empire State building, visited Greenwich Village and, much to the amusement of New Yorkers, we attempted skating in Central Park. We were hardly allowed to spend a cent, so generous was the American hospitality, nonetheless by the end of the week our funds were running low and, with many regrets, we headed north again. David and I now parted company in Montréal, but this time we *did* keep in touch, although it was not until after the war that we again came face-to-face. Back in

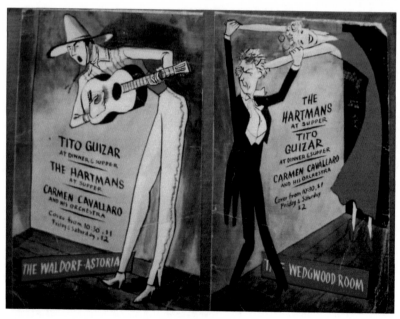

Montréal, I collected my smart new uniform and, very short of cash, I moved to spend the rest of my leave with a delightful cousin in Ottawa. From there I set off, with some trepidation, to Pennfield Ridge in New Brunswick, to be introduced to the Ventura.

PENNFIELD RIDGE

Pennfield Ridge was situated in New Brunswick, in territory which was deeply forested, studded with lakes, and was still in the clutch of winter. Newly qualified pilots, wireless operators and navigators homed in to join the latest course. The first extraordinary procedure was to make up crews, the method used was something akin to a cattle market. All the assorted aircrew assembled in one large room, and at the end of an evening session it was expected that teams of three would be made up. There were Australian, New Zealand and Canadian pilots in abundance, the generally more reticent British were in the minority. I looked at the lists of aircrew and the name Knighton had a friendly feel to it; there was a village of that name near home. It didn't take many minutes to locate Sergeant Jimmy Knighton, and I asked him whether he would consider flying with me? 'Sure thing', he said. I then enquired whether he knew any navigators? 'I share a room with Harry Whiting, a young Englishman, and we get on well. Let's ask him.' Harry agreed, and the apparently impossible task of crewing up was completed, and never did I have cause to regret the choice we made.

There were the usual gloomy tales about the Ventura, of how the Senior Wing Commander had blown himself to pieces attempting a single engine take-off, and how someone had dived straight in from the end of the runway by flipping off the engine switches. There was, no doubt, some truth in these stories; but they had doubtless been embellished by frequent repetition. The Ventura had been developed from the highly successful Hudson, a Coastal Command aircraft of great reliability; it had been assumed that by adding very much more powerful and, of course, heavier engines, the aircraft would fly faster, higher and better than the Hudson. Performance was improved, but at the cost of reliability and the hopelessly in-adequate behaviour on one engine. The engines were enormous 2,000 hp Pratt and Whitney radials.

With a smart new uniform a first salute had to be expected and addressed, and it came from a scruffy young airman who would certainly have been surprised at the embarrassment his salute caused. On that very same day, the Group Captain's car passed some fifty yards away and, of course, I failed to salute. The car stopped and a little man, covered with decorations from 1918, shouted at me, 'Come here, young man! What's your name? You are – I'm sure you're aware – under probation. One word from me and your Commission will be revoked. I am your Commanding Officer; when you see my car with the pennant flying you salute it, even if you are half a mile away. I hope you understand!' Later that evening there was a Mess Dining Night, which I attended, feeling pretty low. After dinner it was decided to play 'High Cockalorum', a lethally dangerous game, which had an object about as pointless as the 'Eton Wall Game'. The Group Captain led one side and his deputy the other. They picked their teams from seasoned members of the mess, until to my astonishment the CO said, 'For my last man, I'll have young Chesterton.' Having earlier wanted to murder him, I suddenly was prepared to die for him, and indeed throughout my course he often found time for a friendly word.

As supposedly trained pilots the emphasis, once we had converted onto the new type, was on operational training. The role of the Ventura was as a low-level fighter bomber, committed to the support of troops on the ground and to shipping strikes. There were two operational squadrons of Venturas forming part of what was known as Two Group in the UK.

Operational training carried on at Pennfield Ridge through February and March. There was a great emphasis on formation flying and low-level cross countries. It was on one such low level flight that Tony Butler had an engine failure about a hundred miles from base. Tony was an experienced pilot, having been instructing on Oxfords for nearly two years. His aircraft would not maintain height, so he skilfully selected a frozen lake amongst the forest trees and made a perfect landing. Fortunately, this was near a logging

Ventura

camp, so he was able to get back to Pennfield Ridge the same day. He was highly commended for his outstanding flying skill. It was decided that the lake was too small for take off if the engine was repaired, and so the aircraft would have to be dismantled and brought back by road using the logging tracks; cranes and transporters were brought to the spot. It was now mid-March. Work started on lifting the engines out, when a crack in the ice appeared, followed by ear splitting sounds, which sent everyone racing to the lake shore. Aircraft, engines, cranes, transporters and lorries all subsided gently below the ice. There had to be a court of inquiry. Poor Tony Butler was kept back nearly six months and although he was completely exonerated, it was a wretched hold up for him. The last third of the course was dedicated to low-level bombing and air firing, this took place from a satellite airfield at a small place called Yarmouth in Nova Scotia.

Pennfield Ridge was situated close to the American border, indeed, there was a bridge nearby which linked New Brunswick with Maine in the United States. The sale of alcohol in the Maritime Provinces was severely restricted; a constant stream of pedestrians was to be seen crossing the border to buy their alcohol in the little town of Calais on the other side of the frontier.

Small practice bombs were used in training and low-level targets were marked out by large white crosses painted on the coastal rocks. These simulated attacks were entertaining; I remember one such occasion, when we were making our attack, as I thought very low, when a Ventura actually homed in on the target well beneath us. Similar targets were used for air firing. The Ventura had two forward firing ·5mm machine guns as well as a twin gun turret. On one gunnery practice, the foreword firing guns jammed, they were in the nose of the aircraft, and nothing could be done to free them. A rather heavy landing cleared the blockage and hundreds of rounds of ammunition were sprayed over Yarmouth. I awaited with dread, picturing a line of people at a bus stop, all mown down, but happily, the bullets must have found their way harmlessly out to sea.

The airfield was shared with a small unit from the Fleet Air Arm. A tiny part of the runway was used by them, for simulated landings as if on the deck of an aircraft carrier, it made one very grateful to have the luxury of long runways.

Jimmy Knighton, Harry Whiting, and I had smoothly blended together, ready to face the next stage in proceedings, and at the end of April we were posted to yet another holding station, this time in Halifax, Nova Scotia, to await the ship home.

HALIFAX AND HOME

The billets at Y depot, Halifax, were satisfactory; boredom was the real enemy, hundreds of trained aircrew from all over Canada were simply waiting for a ship. It was while I was here that I experienced my only true blind date. A party had been made up one evening, and one of the girls said she would find me a partner. Lizzie and I didn't get off to a great start, since she greeted me, 'Wot's cookin good-lookin?' She was pseudo-blonde, wore the skimpiest of clothes and had lipstick that glistened in the light. The party started in someone's room at the Lord Nelson Hotel – there were no public bars in New Brunswick. I stuck it for an hour and then suggested to Lizzie that she might like a taxi to take her home. She jumped at the idea, and so happily ended a ghastly evening.

We were there a month. Our ship was originally French, the *Louis Pasteur,* designed as a luxury liner for the north Atlantic route. She had been fitting out at Le Havre when France fell; a skeleton crew had sailed her to England where she had been converted into a troopship, but she was still reasonably comfortable. Like the *Queen Mary* she never sailed in convoy, but relied on speed to thwart the U-boats. The usual prophets of gloom and doom had stories of the crew on the outward journey being issued with firearms, to control the troops in case of panic, in the unusually rough weather. We had no such experience.

As young officers, we were all given certain responsibilities; in charge of lifeboats, gun crews, mess-decks and so on. I was made baggage officer, this I thought was something of a sinecure, since all the baggage was in the hold.

The ship travelled at great speed and, as we had on the outward journey, we raced up into the Arctic Circle. The voyage took just over a week. I had been away almost exactly a year, and was wildly excited at the prospect of coming back; about halfway across, the wireless began to pick up the strains of Victor Sylvester's orchestra, I felt we were nearly home.

We docked in Liverpool, and I then discovered that the baggage officer, with his accompanying sergeant, had to see all the hold baggage, about 2,000 items, through Customs. This would be a formality we were told – but not so. As the bags, cases and kit bags were being unloaded onto the quay, a very senior Customs officer with gold rings all the way up his arm appeared on the scene. 'Every single item is to be inspected.' He said. Six hours later he left the scene. About half the baggage had been passed, tens of thousands of cigarettes and dozens of bottles of Bourbon had been confiscated, but then, with the departure of the officious gentleman, all remaining bags were nodded through and loaded on a train destined for Harrogate.

The baggage sergeant (a young Canadian) and I travelled together, and the train took us on the beautiful journey over the Pennines; he couldn't believe it. 'I thought England was all one large town', he said. I had managed one brief phone call home and, very exhausted, arrived in Harrogate late in the evening, only to find that I should have been sent to Bournemouth. So the next day I was on my travels again, rather a relief, because I escaped the inevitable complaints about the Customs' confiscations; they never caught up with me.

BOURNEMOUTH

Bournemouth was a holding station with a difference, and we were billeted in what had been the five star Royal Bath Hotel. When we arrived the town was still smarting from a low level raid by sixteen FW 190s about a fortnight earlier; 80 civilians had been killed and 20 Canadian aircrew – their billet had been the Metopolitan Hotel, which had received a direct hit. As if this was not enough, within the first week of our arrival, it was reported that nine Venturas had been shot down on an operation over Brest; then, within days, only one Ventura returned from a similar raid, the captain of that aircraft received a VC. It was something of a relief when we heard that the Venturas were to be withdrawn from front-line service. It was, after all, too slow, carried a small bomb load, and was useless on one engine.

It was an understandable feature of the Royal Air Force that once personnel were channelled in a particular direction that is where they stayed. The Ventura trained crews were scheduled for 2 Group, so to 2 Group they must go. Now that the Ventura was out, the three aircraft left in the Group were Mosquitoes, Mitchells and Bostons. It was now a matter of awaiting conversion on to one of these aircraft types. The wait was a long one.

The powers that be did everything they could to fill the waiting days with interest. There were night vision tests, there were instructional films, there were propaganda films, then everyday for weeks John Mills appeared in a 'Careless Talk Costs Lives' short film, each time it appeared it was greeted with jeers. Probably the most interesting occupation was clay pigeon shooting. This took place on the top of the cliffs. The instructor was a remarkable man, with only one arm; in his demonstrations I never saw him miss with either barrel. The theory was that aiming off to hit the skeets was in principle the same as aiming off to hit an enemy aircraft. My success rate was abysmal. It was no problem getting leave, the obvious understanding was that there could be an immediate recall at any time. So, having been engaged for over a year I reckoned it was time for a wedding.

WEDDING BELLS

On my arrival in Bournemouth from Canada I immediately arranged, with some trepidation, a reunion with my fiancé in the public park three days before my 21st birthday. Happily, all was well. We met frequently thereafter, often for a treasured hour. It was made clear to me that I would be in Bournemouth for at least six weeks.

Above, K's leave pass.

Left, the cheapest honeymoon on record!

24th July 1943.

'Let's get married', I sprung on her. Happily K thought this was a marvellous idea. Tactlessly, I never asked her mother, she would have said 'No!' anyway. I arranged for the banns of marriage to be read the very next Sunday in her local church at Compton near Winchester. Poor Jessie (K's mother) nearly fell out of her seat and was, initially, furious, but then generously gave way.

At breakneck speed, the wedding was organised. K applied for compassionate leave. 'What you mean,' said the bitchy woman in charge of her outfit, 'is *Passionate Leave,* you can add 36 hours to the 48 hour pass to which you are entitled.' I, the intrepid pilot, was told I could have 14 days, or more if I wanted it!

The wedding was a low-key affair, with my father taking the service, there were twelve of us there and it was nine days after my 21st birthday. K and I crammed into a packed train, and then stayed three happy days together at the Norfolk Hotel in Bournemouth, my bill was £7-15s-10d. I then went home to spend the rest of my leave while my wife went back to work!

FINMERE

The frustrating, but enjoyable, idleness in Bournemouth came to a finish near the end of August 1943. As expected, we went for conversion onto the North American Mitchell, at Finmere in Rutland. The Mitchell was a superlative light bomber, it seemed to have no vices; it didn't swing on take off, and with it's tricycle undercarriage it was a joy to land, and it also had an excellent single engine performance. Perhaps it lacked something in speed, and the crew compartments were separated by the bomb bay, which made movement inside the aircraft difficult. Comfortable seats, an efficient heating system and even ashtrays, made it very different from British designs (not that I ever allowed smoking in any aircraft that I flew.) Tiny Shaw joined us as a gunner at this stage. Formerly a butcher, he was tall, strong and, I think, the most even tempered person I ever met. He was a joy, and we were very lucky the day he joined the crew.

The course only lasted a month and included all the usual exercises; bombing, formation flying and single-engine flying, on top of the inevitable circuits and bumps. Night flying came last, and my delightful instructor, Flight Lieutenant Pengelly, saw a couple of landings and then sent us off on a night cross country. During our absence a violent, freak thunderstorm centred itself over Finmere; we came back into the circuit to the accompaniment of horrendous lightning, we were given permission to land, the turbulence was too violent for comfort, but the well mannered Mitchell responded so smoothly that we landed without any problem. All the other aircraft on the exercise were diverted elsewhere. Meanwhile, a white faced Pengelly rushed out to the aircraft. 'Well done', he said, 'I shall see that you get a green endorsement in your log book, a superb piece of flying.' I never had the endorsement, but it was decent of him just the same.

Mitchell

Stoney Cross

Early in the war it had been decided to build up a considerable airborne force; a brigade of parachutists and two divisions of transported men. Training of the troops went on apace; gliders were designed and developed, the most notable of the gliders was the Horsa which could carry twenty-four fully-equipped men. These gliders were largely made in factories, like Parker Knoll, better known for their furniture. Not enough thought had been given to the fundamental task of towing these gliders. True, there was 46 Group, equipped with that wonderfully versatile aircraft (which towed gliders with ease) the Dakota, even so, this machine had two major limitations, it had no defensive armament, and it was not equipped with self-sealing petrol tanks. The twin engined Albermarle had been developed, but it was seriously underpowered and, although it did valiant service, it was not ideal and was eventually withdrawn after D-Day. Then, somewhere in the Air Ministry, some busybody remembered that there were some fifty odd, highly powered Venturas; and, not only were there the aircraft, but the crews trained to fly them. So 38 Group was formed and the suitability of the Ventura for glider towing was tested. The unreliability of the engines, and the fact that the airframes stretched, proved them to be totally unsuitable. The crews, however, had been gathered at an airfield in the New Forest, close to where William Rufus met his death nearly a thousand years before, this bleak site was Stoney Cross. The design of the aerodrome, based one supposes, on the principle of dispersal, was hideously impractical. All the domestic quarters were on one side of the airfield and everything related to flying was three miles away around the perimeter. Awaiting the decision on the Ventura as a glider tug, the crews were involved in what was called continuation training, about twenty hours per crew was spread over three months. This meant that weekend passes, and days off, were readily available.

Some sort of personal transport was almost essential. For the cost of £10·00 I invested in a motorbike. I bought a fairly elderly, 350cc AJS from a garage some ten miles away. The garage owner was somewhat concerned that I had never before ridden a motorcycle. He persuaded me to ride to the end of the road, which was dead straight for two miles, and return for his assessment. He was satisfied that I was safe, but anxiously advised me not to try out the machine's paces until I was fully confident, but he failed to warn me to tuck all flapping garments out of the way. It was, I suppose, inevitable that, a few miles down the road, I should see what speed I could coax out of the old machine. One moment, I was in the saddle, the next, I was bouncing along the road on my backside, the bike went weaving on until it finished in a ditch a hundred yards ahead. Neither bike nor I were damaged, but my raincoat, which had caught in the chain, was ripped in half and my trousers had a neat triangular tear. I removed the remains of my raincoat, restarted the engine with one kick, and returned to Stoney Cross at a sober pace.

The next morning, I rode the three miles round the camp to visit the camp tailor to have my trousers repaired. On leaving him, I couldn't restart the bike so tried to get it going down a slope by letting in the clutch, it roared into life and, for the second time in twenty-four hours, it raced away from me. The bike ran into a tree and rolled on its side unhurt, and I fell on my face to ruin another pair of trousers. The tailor laughed his head off and said, 'I'd better repair one pair for you straightaway, so you have something to wear!'

The news that the Ventura was considered unfit for glider towing surprised none of us, and well founded rumours filtered through, that the Short Stirling had been tested for such duties and found suitable; it was, I suppose, an inevitable sequence that all 38 Group crews should be trained to fly them.

'Bomber Harris' had built up a formidable bomber force, but was finding that the casualties sustained on his Stirling squadrons were unacceptable. The Stirling could not make effective altitude with a full bomb load, making them vulnerable both to attack by fighters and medium level flak, so these squadrons were being re-equipped with Lancasters. Thus, the Stirling became available for 38 Group, it was not ideal for glider towing, but it was the best yet and, by stripping out the mid-upper turret, it was adapted to carry paratroops.

The Stirling was the first, and largest, of the four engined bombers. The original design in the period shortly before the war had been for an aircraft of 110 foot wing span. The Air Ministry insisted that this should be reduced to 99 feet, so the aircraft would fit into the hangers built at RAF stations, which were of a standard size. This extraordinary demand was met, but, in doing so, very much reduced the capabilities of this remarkable aeroplane; but more of this later. Proof, if proof was needed that conversion onto Stirlings was imminent, came when each of the crews received an extra member, nominally a bomb-aimer, but actually a jack of all trades. Doug Smith, formerly a flower grower from the Scilly Isles, joined us and immediately settled down, he proved to be a happy addition to the crew.

Christmas was approaching, and the Officers Mess committee decided to have a party. The scale of this rather got out of hand,

and developed to become a Mess Ball. Since so many of the officers came from the Commonwealth, indeed, they far outnumbered the British, it was decided to approach the naval authorities in Portsmouth to see if a party of Wrens might be invited to act as partners for are all these young men. There seemed to be no shortage of volunteers.

The regular officers were resplendent in their mess kit. The rest of us wore white shirts and bow ties with our best uniform. The Station dance band was signed-on for the evening, and very good they were. The only alcoholic beverage readily available was rum, and large quantities of a powerful rum punch were prepared. The mess was splendidly decorated and the Ball proved to be a wow. K had managed to squeeze a 36 hour pass from her miserly officers, and we booked in for the night at a pub in Romsey, about 10 miles down the road. The Ball was due to end at 1·00am, and the RN transport duly arrived to pick up their charges, but half the Wrens were missing; some of them were only rounded up some two hours later, indeed, several couples had to be routed out of Venturas on the airfield, which had made convenient nesting boxes. There was the most terrible row and, I suppose, it was fortuitous that only two days later, all Ventura crews were posted away. Two weddings followed a few weeks later, so the Ball can be said to have had a happy ending.

Tilstock

Early in 1944, we were posted to a Heavy Conversion Unit in Tilstock, this was a unit known as 1665 HCU. It was typical of dispersed wartime RAF stations, it comprised a variety of nissen huts, of various shapes and sizes, widely scattered in the woods. It was nearly a mile from the domestic huts to the 'messes' and at least another mile to the 'flights'. The aircraft on the unit were redundant Stirling 1s and 111s. The Stirling was in many respects an aircraft well ahead of its time, greater use of electrics was made than on most aircraft of that period, and the Stirling 1 was fitted with hydraulic controls to the engines, these linkages were so complicated that they never proved satisfactory, and were abandoned in favour of cable controls on later marks. The serviceability, particularly of the mark 1s, was, to say the least, dodgy.

It was here that we were joined by the sixth member of our crew, the flight engineer; he was well qualified, but very nervous and would never let us take to the air in an aircraft which he considered was not in perfect condition, unless he was forced to do so; a hopelessly impractical approach with these rather ancient

Just crewed up at Tilstock, left to right: Harry Whiting, Jimmy Knighton, Johnie Ecart, George Chesterton, Tiny Shaw, Doug Smith.

aircraft. Johnie Ecart was his name, and he fitted into our jolly team rather less well than all the others.

The conversion course took the form of a fortnight's lectures and ground training, followed by another two weeks flying training, concentrated into about 25 hours in the air, about half of which was at night.

On the night of the 31st of January 1944, I was detailed with my crew to carry out five circuits and landings. The detail began at 6.00pm, but the first two aircraft we climbed into proved to be hopelessly unserviceable; the first with an unacceptable magneto drop and the next with faulty brakes, the third one, 'K-King', was by no means perfect, but I overruled Johnie Ecart, considering it fit for circuits and bumps. It was now after 7.00pm and the other aircraft in the detail were just finishing their quota of landings. The runway in use was lit by old-fashioned goose neck flares, which had to be put in place by hand, one by one. At 6.00pm there had been a fresh breeze, blowing directly down the runway, which was one of the two shorter ones. By 7.00pm the wind was shifting, and by the time we came to do our last landing after about an hour's flying it was directly across the 800 yard landing strip. The control tower called to say that the flares could be moved over to the long runway, but it would take at least an hour, which, understandably, they were reluctant to do, but if we landed at once we could finish the detail. Down we came on the final approach, the wind had now a fairly strong tailwind element, and, instead of being a few feet above the ground at the beginning of the runway, we must have been at least 50 feet above it, and with the throttle fully closed the great Stirling wallowed on. Touchdown came with only 200 yards of runway left, beyond this was a 200 yard grass overshoot area before the main Whitchurch Road, which was protected by two banks. The engines were cut to the accompaniment of jets of flame from the exhaust as unused petrol ignited. Still K-King rumbled on, halfway across the overshoot strip the tail was down, but there was no hope of stopping before the road. A bus trundled past, happily out of range and unaware of the narrowness of its escape, as the heavy Stirling crashed through first one bank, then over the road to demolish the other, and it still had enough momentum to flatten two large chicken houses. K-King finally came to rest, towering above the chicken farmers bungalow in a dense storm of feathers and to the accompaniment of indignant squawks from a thousand frightened hens. From the control tower came the advice, 'Alright K-King you may back track!' Surprisingly, the aircraft was undamaged and the whole episode was put down to inexperience; we were flying again the next night.

FAIRFORD AND OPERATIONS

Exactly two years after my arrival in London in February 1942, I was, at last, posted to an operational squadron. 190 Squadron had been disbanded in 1919 and was now reformed, over 20 years later, at Leicester East. We were only there a month before moving to the newly built Fairford. The layout here was typical of wartime airfields, widely dispersed nissen huts, and, wherever possible, use had been made of the natural camouflage from trees. 'D' site, where I lived, lay at the bottom of a slope; it was damp in winter and plagued by insects in summer, particularly during one fortnight when there was an invasion of earwigs. The only salvation from these wretched things was to stand each bed leg in cocoa or tobacco tins half filled with water, even this was no defence from those which dropped from the roof. I remember a biologist in the hut informing us that the female of the species had curved pincers, and the male straight ones, like a pair of pliers, or was it the other way round? We were delighted when, one morning, they were no more. In the winter it was possible to raise a moderate degree of warmth. The other occupants of hut number 14 were from either Australia or New Zealand, and all aircrew; it is hard to imagine a more resourceful combination. The camp coke store, with its thousands of tons of this valuable commodity, was within easy reach, but was protected by a strong, ten foot high fence. There were threats of hideous penalties, even court martial, for anyone appropriating extra coke.

No one was court-martialled and our bucket was never empty. On the coldest nights our 'tortoise' stove stood in the middle of the hut, giving a comfortable red glow into the small hours.

The only place on the station with baths was the WAAF site, strictly out of bounds to all males, except at special bath times. On Tuesday and Thursday afternoons, between 4·00 and 6·00pm, there was a period set aside for officers. No doubt other times were allocated to lesser mortals. Tuesday was the day that suited me, and after tea I would go through a weekly ritual. Towel and soap were obvious necessities, an old penny or half crown with a flannel less obvious, but essential. Not an Air Force bath in the kingdom, so it seemed, had a plug. However, a large coin, wrapped in a flannel and assisted by the judicious use of a heel, made most baths watertight. One Tuesday, a little later than usual, I found my way to the bathhouse and settled down for a glorious soak. The soporific atmosphere soon saw me asleep. I woke in horror and near panic to hear girlish voices around me. Fortunately the partitions were high, and happily I had chosen a cubicle with a window. No one has ever leapt quicker from a bath, nor dressed at such speed to slide noiselessly from the window and slip away to freedom and safety.

Before leaving Stoney Cross I had sold my motorbike to Doug Smith for a fiver and had acquired a little car. This was a black Morris Minor, which I had bought from a chap who was posted overseas. It was the most wonderful little car, and it was not long before it was adopted by my crew and was known as the 'Flier'. We had a built-in difficulty, that all my crew were NCOs, so our social life together was nearly always off the station, since officers were not normally welcome in the sergeants' mess, and vice versa.

Officers had use of their mess, where many peacetime traditions were carefully preserved. We did not, of course, have batmen, but each hut was allocated a couple of WAAFs, who made our beds, cleaned our shoes and buttons, and even brought us tea in the morning – positive luxury.

There were two Stirling squadrons at Fairford, 190 and 620, each one was divided into two flights, with 12 aircraft in each. The main role of the squadrons was to work closely with the airborne forces, this meant endless training, exercises and practices. The secondary role was of almost equal importance, this was the supply of all sorts of ammunition, weapons and supplies to resistance movements, most especially in France, and these operations came under the umbrella of SOE (Special Operations Executive), all highly secret, and the operations nearly always took place during periods of full moon.

| Frank Pascoe | George Chesterton | Sandy Anderson | John Hay | John Gilliard |

It was accepted that each crew had loose possession of a particular aircraft, this was a very unofficial arrangement and no crew had a positive right of ownership, but it did mean that the air crews and ground crews worked closely together. My aircraft was LK431, and its recognition letter was F; we knew it as 'Ferdinand el Taurus' and we had a picture of a bull painted on the nose. Another advantage was that each aircraft, rather like a car, had its own special characteristics, which ground and flying crews came to know and gain confidence over by working together. Our ground crew was led by a redheaded Lancastrian Flight Sergeant, known to us as 'Ginger'. He was the salt of the earth, nothing was too much trouble for him, and, for example, the Flier was seldom short of petrol; the little car did go like a bomb on a hundred octane fuel.

Exercises and training went on apace. One of the characteristics of Stirlings was a tendency to swing violently to starboard on take-off, this had to be anticipated by judicious use of the throttles, but an advantage of glider towing was that the swing was masked by the weight of the glider. Towing a glider had many of the characteristics of a car pulling a trailer, violent movements had to

Jimmy Knighton   Doug Smith

be avoided, and the rope needed to be kept taut at all times. The early ropes were made of hemp, but then nylon came in, and the new ones were more resilient and stronger. There was a primitive communication line encased in the rope, this seldom worked with any efficiency and instructions had to be bellowed for any chance of comprehension. The ropes were of

Tiny Shaw

considerable value, and after each practice had to be collected, so there was a special dropping zone, marked with a white cross. On one black day, two aircraft from 620 Squadron collided in the dropping zone, both plummeted to earth, and there were no survivors. The two hideous black columns of smoke, which billowed into the air only half a mile from the airfield, haunt me to this day. This ghastly accident put a blight

Harry Whiting

on the whole Station for weeks. About an hour after the collision, I was walking into the mess when a friend from 620 saw me and, turning white as a sheet, said, 'My God, George, I was just told that you were flying one of those aircraft,' and, as the colour came back into his cheeks, he added, 'I do apologise, seeing you was an amazing shock and, of course, a very happy one!'

S.O.E. The Special Operations Executive

The Special Operations Executive was a small, tough British Secret Service 'dirty tricks' department, set up in 1940. Its job was to support and stimulate resistance in the occupied countries. The total strength, worldwide, was never more than 10,000 men and 3,200 women. There was a branch of the Executive in every country occupied by the Germans and Japanese.

In the European sector most of the agents, couriers and wireless operators were trained in Britain. Many aspects of their training remain secret to this day, knowledge of them would be invaluable to terrorists. The SOE training was demanding and exhaustive. Nearly all the agents showed a quite staggering courage, very rarely there were those who treacherously became double agents. So skilful were the Germans at interrogation that many of the unfortunate numbers captured inadvertantly gave away information, often with disastrous results.

Early in 1944, as I have already mentioned, 38 Group of the Royal Air Force was founded. Ten different squadrons were sited at five separate stations. Each of the squadrons was equipped with Stirlings, with the idea of practising a dual role; SOE operations and work with airborne troops. Since 1940, 161 Squadron and 138 Squadron had operated from Tempsford; these were the real cloak and dagger boys, specialising in actually landing agents in France and Holland. They operated principally with Hudsons and Lysanders. The introduction of 38 Group Stirlings enormously increased the volume of supplies that could be dropped in preparation for D-Day. The Stirling, now redundant from Bomber Command, was the ideal aircraft for SOE since it comfortably carried a load of 24 containers, and also four large panniers. During the full moon period, which lasted about ten days each month, there must have been dozens of Stirlings flying at low level over much of the continent.

The containers most usually used were just over a foot in diameter, 5ft. 9in. long, and had four carrying handles. Their weight was about 2cwt; they were dropped by parachute. The normal loads consisted mostly of small arms; Sten guns, ammunition, grenades, plastic explosives and anti-tank mortars called 'Piats' were all dropped. (Over a million Stens were parachuted). It was policy not to drop larger weapons, but agents, through their wireless operators, made shopping lists which were supplied if possible. The packing of the containers was developed to a fine art. It was said that they were so skilfully filled that, once unpacked in the field, it was virtually impossible to fit all the items back. The odd space would be filled with such goodies as coffee, tobacco and even, sometimes, a pair of socks. Radio sets were occasionally dropped in lined and padded panniers.

Dropping zones were carefully selected by the agents, who would arrange with SOE where and when the drop should be made, and make any special requests known; this would set the whole machinery in motion, culminating in the selection of a crew to carry out a particular drop. Sadly, the site of the drop zone was sometimes betrayed to the enemy. Almost certainly, on one of our drops in France, the reception party was ambushed; a brief firefight took place in which the Resistance party stood little chance. The only thing we could do was to return home and report the dismal news. Infiltration of resistance cells was patchy, and was possibly worst in Holland. The most disappointing and frustrating thing was to reach a drop zone and either find no one there or, worst of all, have no correct identification letters given – this meant that the load had to be brought home.

The best work carried out by the amazingly brave resistance groups was usually sabotage. One of the most spectacular examples being the Norwegian sabotage of the German heavy water plant in Norway. This great feat was romanticised in the film *The Heroes of Telemark.* Another, less spectacular, example was the sabotaging of two long trains of tank transport wagons for German Tiger tanks. Just after D-Day, these trains were being loaded in the South of France so the tanks could be rushed to the beachheads. The local resistance had asked for a consignment of carbarundum; a substance which has quite the reverse effect of lubricating oil. The carbarundum was substituted for oil in the bearings of the railway wagons, which then seized up within a mile. As a result, the tanks were delayed from the battlefront by seventeen days. Transport sabotage was one of the most effective ways resistance groups could upset enemy plans; even altering railway points could cause traffic chaos.

It was one of the roles of 38 Group to keep the resistance fighters supplied with the essentials for guerrilla war.

INSIDE THE STIRLING

The crew of a Stirling used to enter the aircraft by a door on the left-hand, or port side, near the tail. There was a three rung aluminium stepladder, which took members of the crew into the aircraft, and on the right it was a short step towards the Rear Gunner's turret; there was a place for him to hang his parachute before he entered the turret, which had two steps for him to clamber up. He was equipped with a special electrical suit, which was essential to keep him warm because he was right out on a limb. Turning left from the door, there was a clear area before a steepish incline, which indicated the large bomb bay underneath. It was quite easy to walk over this until the main spar was reached; this was an enormous structure carrying the whole weight of the wings, and had to be crawled through. At about this point was the position of the Flight Engineer. He had a reasonably comfortable seat and a whole battery of instruments for all the engines and, most importantly, gauges to indicate the fuel levels for all the different tanks. Beyond him was the position of the Wireless Operator; he had a table and, of course, a bucket type chair, and in front of him the various radio sets, which were the particular tools of his trade. Continuing forward, there was probably the most comfortable position of all, that of the Navigator. He could curtain himself away from the rest of the world, with his navigating table in front of him, which became more and

The flight deck of a Stirling:
the lever to the right of the throtles was the glider release.

more cluttered with radar instruments as time moved on. His position was also the warmest in the aircraft, and very often he hardly left his seat from take-off to landing. Moving forward again, a steep step or two up reached the two pilots' seats. The one on the left was that of the Captain, with all the controls and instruments for flying the aircraft, the other pilot's seat had all the essential controls but was normally used as the

The wieless operator's station.

home of the Bomb Aimer. Proceeding down into the nose of the aircraft there were several steps down and then a flat area for the bomb aimer to lie prone, and a large area of clear perspex which was invaluable for map reading purposes.

In the Royal Air Force it was traditional for the pilot to be the Captain of the aircraft; strangely, this could mean a Sergeant pilot captaining an aircraft which might include several officers in the crew. In my crew there was really nothing unusual, because I was the only officer. The crew in one of these aircraft were totally interdependent, in other words, we relied on each other. Each member of the crew was supposed to have a working knowledge of the tasks of other members of the team so that in emergency there would not be a total breakdown, but it was impossible to grasp all the specialist knowledge of the navigator, wireless operator, engineer and rear gunner. From the moment of take-off there would be no contact with anyone outside the aircraft; this was clearly for simple security reasons. Messages could be received in the aircraft by the wireless operator and passed on. The only time silence could be broken was in the case of an emergency when a distress signal could be sent out. There was on all RAF aircraft an ingenious and useful device known as 'IFF', this stood for 'identification friend or foe'. It was switched on when approaching the friendly coast and recorded a signal, which identified the aircraft as friendly to all local defences. A further form of identification was by means of a Verey pistol signal. The pistol was charged with a cartridge carrying the pre-arranged colours of the day and, in case of emergency over identification, this could be fired in the hope that those seeing it would then know who we were.

When all the crew were in their appropriate positions aboard the aircraft, they would carry out all the essential checks and tests on their own equipment and would then call into the captain to say that they were ready for take-off. Once in the air, the captain would call round all his crew to make sure that everything was in order and the operation or exercise could go ahead.

First Operation

At last, in the full moon period of April 1944, we went to war. We had to fly down to Tarrant Rushton for briefing, the Operations Room at Fairford was not ready for use. We were detailed to drop 24 containers to a Resistance group near Caen, in Northern France. We took off after dark, but with an enormous moon just rising in the sky. We were fully loaded with 24 containers. We headed roughly south, crossing the Channel at low level; everything went

Dinghy drill in a Cotswold gravel pit. The three on the right hand side of the front dinghy are Tiny Shaw, Harry Whiting and Jack McReady.

like clockwork, courses and tracks were immaculate, WT fixes confirmed our position, as did Gee fixes (early radar). Tiny Shaw, the rear gunner, tested his guns over the Channel and the French coast came into sight. A rapid climb to 10,000 feet to cross the coast just East of Cherbourg followed, and then we descended, equally rapidly, to fly at 500 feet over France. So bright was the moon that the tell-tale glow of the exhausts was scarcely noticeable, and we felt very vulnerable. Almost as though on a quiet exercise, the drop zone came up unmistakably, just south of Caen. On our first approach the identification letters 'AD' were flashed to us and, when we replied, an 'L' shape of torches appeared, as if by magic. Bomb doors open, speed back to 140 knots, 500 feet opposite the first torch, containers away – they floated safely to earth as we made one more circuit before setting off for home. A little lazy flak was seen over the coast, but the return journey was as uneventful as that going out, until a diversion call was received. Tarrant Rushton was under fog and we were sent to Boscombe Down, a strange First World War airfield built over the crown of a hill. We landed safely and taxied the Stirling to park by the control tower. The ground crews were intensely interested as they saw the static lines trailing from the bomb-bay. Despite the threats of a Senior Intelligence Officer, we followed our strict briefing instructions and said nothing apart from, 'Operation successfully completed'. This must have seemed surprising at Boscombe Down, which was one of the most secret airfields in the service! A few days later, a coded message came through to Fairford thanking Flying Officer Chesterton and crew for goods received. Very satisfactory.

The Second Operation

With D-Day more or less imminent, there were endless exercises with airborne troops. After one such exercise, which occupied much of the night and early morning, my flight commander suggested that I take the rest of the day off. I rang K and found she was off-duty, so I dived into the Flier and set off for Middle Wallop. About halfway there I fell sound asleep at the wheel, the nearside front wheel hit a steep bank and the whole car shot into the air, rolled right over and landed on its roof. Needless to say, I woke up pretty smartly and put my arms up to protect my head; they became trapped as the sunshine roof was ripped away. Two old dears looked over a fence and said, quite casually, 'He must be dead.' As calmly as I could, I said, 'I am not dead, would you please find someone to lift the car.' The local schoolmaster and a couple of strong men raised the car and put it back on its wheels; apart from badly grazed forearms, I was unhurt. The schoolmaster had phoned Fairford, and an ambulance arrived for me. I went back sitting next to the driver. The MO was furious, I should have been on a stretcher! He insisted that I should have 48 hours off-duty. What better way of spending it than re-visiting the Flier? The garage that had rescued the car had written it off as scrap. They changed their minds when it leapt into life with the first touch on the starter. It only needed a new windscreen, two new windows, and a roof covering. This was all done within a week, and I collected the Flier, looking better than ever, and was able to fit in an hour or two of cricket coaching for the schoolmaster's two sons.

With the next full moon we went to Tarrant Rushton to be briefed for the next SOE trip. Briefings in the Air Force followed a semi-formal pattern. A senior officer outlined the aims of the operation, followed by an intelligence officer who drew attention to likely areas of flak and enemy activity. The navigation leader would give routes and courses, the signals leader would give call signs, and so on. Usually, the Met. Officer came last, greeted almost invariably with derision, he gave a forecast which included all important wind directions and speeds. This particular operation was to an area south of Limoges and, in contrast to the earlier one, was boringly unsuccessful; there was no reception, although we flew four times round the drop zone, so the containers had to be brought home. On top of this, there was a battery leak, which resulted in the aircraft being filled with noxious fumes. Very unsatisfactory.

Air Tests

Air tests were obligatory when any aircraft had been subjected to major servicing of any kind; it might, for example, be an engine change, or a major or minor inspection. Normally, these tests were part of the daily routine, but, occasionally, there was need for an urgent one. One Tuesday, there had been little happening, so John Gilliard favourably answered my plea to go off and find myself a bath. Baths, as I have said, were made available to officers on two afternoons a week, between 4.00 and 6.00pm on the WAAF Site. Having had my essential bath, I retired to the mess and had a couple of drinks. Gilliard rang the mess and asked whether I would do an Air Test on 'M-Mike' (which had just had an engine change); it was needed as a standby aircraft for that evening's operations. I explained that I'd had a drink or two, but he simply apologised and said that there was no one else available, he went on to say that he had a young supernumary engineer standing by. I set off at once, picking up Jimmy Knighton, my wireless operator, on the way. The three of us were taken out to the aircraft, and we prepared for the test. I was alarmed by the extent to which my vision was affected by the two whiskies I had drunk in the mess, to be honest, I was not fit to fly. I muttered something to Jack McReady, the young engineer, who said, 'Turn the oxygen on.' I followed his advice and was astonished at the way my vision became crystal clear, the instruments positively leapt their information forward. The Air Test then went off without incident. On landing, I approached Gilliard and said, 'Young Sgt. McCready is one in a million. My current engineer is leaving on a Leaders' course, may I please have the new chap in my crew?' So it transpired; a positive red letter day. He was outstanding, a calm, shrewd Scot, whose judgment was always sound and he never, ever, let us down.

There were spare aircraft in the squadron to which no crew had a special attachment. 'H-How' was one such, and it was felt by everyone to be a jinx. It was slow to climb, swung more viciously than most on take-off, and flew left wing low; it was generally unpopular. After a multitude of complaints, Shorts of Belfast sent one of their test pilots to give it a thorough going over. Gilliard spotted me in the crew room and said, 'George, will you sit in the right-hand seat while this chap does his test.' It was an amazing and very alarming experience, from take-off to landing, about an hour later, the test pilot took the most astonishing liberties. He feathered two engines on one side and did a steep turn into them – outrageous, he corkscrewed the aircraft on three engines – monstrous. He dived, climbed and generally threw the poor old Stirling about the sky in a truly remarkable manner. It is hard to believe that there was anything wrong with this jinx aircraft, and indeed the test pilot's report was to this effect, subject to minor aileron adjustments. Even though H-How was given a clean bill of health, it remained the poor relation of the squadron.

D-Day

The two-month period before D-Day saw preparations and training gather in pace. During the full moon periods SOE operations continued, but, by chance, we only carried out one, a particularly frustrating flight to a dropping zone south of Paris. There was no reception of any kind, so we returned with our load, experiencing no significant enemy activity.

One became conscious of the fact that hundreds of thousands of troops were slowly filtering their way south. Down nearly every country lane, units of artillery, squadrons of tanks and an amazing variety of military units were preparing for the great events to come.

SUPREME HEADQUARTERS
ALLIED EXPEDITIONARY FORCE

Soldiers, Sailors and Airmen of the Allied Expeditionary Force!

You are about to embark upon the Great Crusade, toward which we have striven these many months. The eyes of the world are upon you. The hopes and prayers of liberty-loving people everywhere march with you. In company with our brave Allies and brothers-in-arms on other Fronts, you will bring about the destruction of the German war machine, the elimination of Nazi tyranny over the oppressed peoples of Europe, and security for ourselves in a free world.

Your task will not be an easy one. Your enemy is well trained, well equipped and battle-hardened. He will fight savagely.

But this is the year 1944! Much has happened since the Nazi triumphs of 1940-41. The United Nations have inflicted upon the Germans great defeats, in open battle, man-to-man. Our air offensive has seriously reduced their strength in the air and their capacity to wage war on the ground. Our Home Fronts have given us an overwhelming superiority in weapons and munitions of war, and placed at our disposal great reserves of trained fighting men. The tide has turned! The free men of the world are marching together to Victory!

I have full confidence in your courage, devotion to duty and skill in battle. We will accept nothing less than full Victory!

Good Luck! And let us all beseech the blessing of Almighty God upon this great and noble undertaking.

Dwight D Eisenhower

General Eisenhower's letter to the D-Day troops.

As far as our training was concerned, we had almost daily exercises with paratroops or gliders. In April alone, we carried out 16 Horsa glider launches, some at night, and many involving cross-country training. Then there were exercises involving paratroops and the dropping of containers. One of the most exhilarating practices was fighter affiliation, this usually took place over the Bristol Channel. It involved the meeting of a Spitfire, or some other fighter, which would make a series of attacks and our aim was to take evasive action. The Stirling was the most amazing aircraft, nearly every time a fighter attacked it was possible to turn inside it, much to the disgust of the fighter pilots.

As D-Day approached, we all knew that sea and weather conditions had to be as near-perfect as possible. It was made clear that the invasion would have to be made on the fifth, sixth or seventh of June. On the fourth of June all RAF stations were sealed off, this isolation remained until the invasion was actually under way, to all intents and purposes we were confined to camp, we were not permitted either to receive phone calls or to make them. It was about this time that all aircrew were summoned to Fairford's newly opened Operations Room to be addressed by a very senior Staff Officer. We received a pep talk, well-intentioned, but abysmally delivered; we were told that 50% casualties were expected, whatever happened, we were to press on with our task. His talk was not well received.

The role of most 38 Group Stirlings was to deliver paratroops of the Sixth Airborne Division, Fifth Parachute Brigade, onto the eastern banks of the river Orne. They were to be dropped two hours ahead of the seaborne invasion; the object was to secure the Allied left flank. Lengthy briefings were held, with remarkable models

Lined up for D-Day

and photographs of the dropping zones on display. The weather deteriorated, so the invasion was delayed 24 hours. This of course meant an agonising wait, endless games of rounders were played on the tarmac, and even a primitive Test match was organised, regrettably won by the Australians – again!

A window of opportunity appeared on the weather charts and General Eisenhower gave the go-ahead. It was normally policy for the aircrew not to meet their charges until the last minute, but over the 24-hour delay we had made some contacts, and we had met our 'load' of two officers, a remarkable Sergeant Major and a fine looking group of young paratroops. The aircraft of both 620 and 190 Squadrons were lined-up, ready to go, and after final briefings the paratroopers marched to their allotted aircraft. We had only 18, but they carried considerable quantities of radar kit to set up and establish on landing. Although it was an hour short of midnight, being midsummer, it was not oppressively dark.

The signal came to start up. We were in our own aircraft, *Ferdinand el Taurus*, newly painted with its special D-Day white stripes. The Bristol Hercules was a remarkable engine, always easy to start. A signal to one of the ground crew, and we started the engines, starboard inner first, then port inner, port outer and, finally, starboard outer. A quick run up of the engines, and we were taxiing clumsily towards take-off. A green light, and we were away. The two starboard throttles had to go wide open to check any swing, until the tail came up and full rudder control was possible. We roared down the runway and left the ground at just over 120kts, up with the enormous undercarriage, wound in slowly by electric motors, and away to France with a course given by Harry. We crossed over the Channel at only 1,000 feet, making a rapid climb to cross the enemy coast between 8 and 10,000 feet, there was some desultory flak, but very little opposition as we slipped down towards the dropping zone. Harry and Doug were convinced that we were right on course, so we descended to 800 feet and slowed

Above: D-Day take-off. Below: Stirling EF433

to 140 kts, the main door was opened, the red light went on and, seconds later, on with the green and the whole stick of paratroops left in quick succession. Tiny, in the rear turret, reported that all were safely away. He thought he saw the first few safely reach the ground. It was time to turn for home. On the return journey, we had the spectacular sight of the invasion fleet making its way to the Normandy coast. Ships of every type, size and description stretched across the Channel – only just visible as it was still hardly past midnight. The return flight was uneventful. The aircrew bus picked us up from dispersal and dropped us opposite the new operations room. I ran towards the entrance and slap into a coil of barbed wire, which, I swear, had just been put in place. I gashed the back of my right hand. I went through debriefing dripping large quantities of blood. I was then persuaded that I should go to Sick Quarters for some sort of dressing. The MO roared with laughter, put a great bandage on and said, 'You will have a D-Day

Above: Stirling 'Ferdinand el Taurus'

scar to show off to your grandchildren.' When John Gilliard, my flight commander, saw me next morning, he too laughed and said, 'You can't fly with that great bandage, so you might as well take the day off.' I sought out the Flier which, thanks to Ginger my flight sergeant, was always ready to go. We were no longer confined to camp, so I set off to Middle Wallop to see K.

I drove to Middle Wallop and picked up K who had been on duty through all the excitement of D-Day. After the first shock of seeing the enormous bandage on my right hand, K laughed like everyone else, we then happily spent the day together. I returned to Fairford driving against a constant stream of military traffic moving to the south coast ports. Back at Fairford, I immediately had my bandage replaced by a plaster, and was back to normal.

D-Day, before take-off.

Two days after D-Day, we were briefed to resupply some of the paratroops who had not yet met up with the main force. Surprisingly, there was very little flak, indeed, the only problem we experienced was from a sniper with a machine gun on a church spire, we circled round so that Tiny could have a good shot at him. The sniper disappeared, showing, I suspect, that discretion was the better part of valour. Our return journey was uneventful.

620 Squadron Stirlings.

A Stirling IV dropping containers; note, the third parachute did not open.

Full Moon

Following the success of D-Day, there was hectic activity with the many French Resistance units. The full moon periods of July and August were particularly busy. No operation was routine, there was always tension and suspense, although, post D-Day, the crossing of the enemy coast was relieved of some anxiety.

An operation code-named 'Grog' was in the Brest area; the Germans were putting up a particularly stubborn defence on the Cherbourg Peninsula and supplies to the Resistance were important. The intelligence briefing warned of large units of the US fleet offshore; they had the reputation of being very trigger happy. We safely dropped our load of 24 containers, and set course for home. There was a shattering explosion which, at first, I felt was a direct hit on the tail; the aircraft was thrown out of control, but only momentarily. Immediately, Doug was directed to fire-off the colours of the day – a Verey pistol was always loaded for this purpose – and then Jimmy was instructed to send out a May Day call. Happily, it was possible to cancel this, since full control of the aircraft soon became possible. Tiny asked to come forward since the door of his rear turret was partly jammed and it was not opening as it should. Next morning, our ground crew Flight Sergeant, Ginger, asked us to go down to the flights; he showed us that the rear turret was now attached by one bolt – all the others had been blasted off by what had, undoubtedly, been an American shell. However, in fairness to them, we were possibly out of position.

Three nights later, we were south of the Loire. The captain's personal remarks on the Intelligence Report read as follows, 'Very successful trip. Flashing of letter 'P' in very good pauses, and a line of bonfires, made for a satisfactory run in and drop. The drop zone was identified visually, and the position confirmed by Gee. Drop made at 500 feet at 150 knots, 24 containers and 2 packages were delivered.' Two nights later, we were back in the Brest area. On this operation, Jack McReady became our official engineer; his baptism was a lively one. Close to the dropping zone, there was a fiercely defended dam; the Germans were, by now, aggressively sensitive in such areas, we were caught by searchlights. I remembered Biggles' advice, 'Never look out of the cockpit at a searchlight, you will be blinded'. Tiny opened up with his guns and out went the lights, we all gave him credit for sharp shooting. Just to keep Jack on his toes, the starboard outer engine had to be feathered (shut down), and we returned home with some relief. This was followed by an amazing operation in which nearly every 38 group Stirling was involved. On a plateau near the Swiss border, an enormous bonfire was lit to indicate the drop zone and although it was enveloped in cloud we were permitted, on this occasion, to drop over the red glow of the fire. Only too often the worst enemy was the weather. Towards the end of August a hideous thunderstorm prevented any hope of landing at Fairford, we diverted to Holmesley South. Three days later, a drop zone near Geneva was totally covered in cloud, and we had to bring our load home.

In addition to SOE operations, there were occasional SAS trips which involved direct contact with British commandos, sometimes actually dropping the troops.

On the lighter side, the wives of both the Wing Commander and John Gilliard, our Flight Commander, were in Cornwall and both expecting babies. Flights to Port Reath and St Eval, under the guise of continuation training, appear in our log books providing happy interludes before the horrors of Arnhem.

TINY SHAW

This is Tiny Shaw's version of the story over the Cherbourg Peninsula.

My story happened in August 1944. We flew on an SOE operation over France and were warned-off flying over the Cherbourg Peninsula as the Americans were involved in heavy fighting there; all aircraft flying over would be treated as hostile. On the return flight, after a successful drop, an engine on the Stirling developed a fault and had to be closed down, which caused great vibration on the fuselage, especially at the rear. The skipper and Dougie, the Bomb Aimer, had great difficulty in flying the aircraft. The most direct way home was across the Peninsula. We met heavy 'Ack Ack', presumably from the Americans, despite firing the colours of the day. We had some very near misses, one of which blew the lower escape hatch in. The skipper warned us to be prepared to bail out. My 'chute was strapped to the rear of the aircraft in the fuselage behind the gun turret. After centralising the turret, I found the doors had jammed. With help from Jimmy, the Wireless Operator, we managed to free them. Happily, we did not have to jump. I decided to fly with the turret doors left open – in case they jammed again. I found it very cold and draughty. After a time, a thought crossed my mind. I passed it on to the rest of the crew, asking if they knew that it was Friday the 13th. The replies over the intercom, were, as might be expected, unprintable. I had always had a warped sense of humour. Happily, we returned safely.

The following morning, I was sent for, to the hangar where 'F' for Fox was having an engine change and service. The armoury sergeant then showed me where the bolts securing the gun-turret to the aircraft had all sheared off, except one, owing to the vibration. Since then I have never considered Friday the 13th as being unlucky.

Operation Market Garden

There was a feeling of optimism and excitement when the plans for Market Garden were made known. It was to be the largest ever airborne operation, and the object was to capture three bridges over the Rhine at Eindhoven, Nijmegan and Arnhem, aiming to bring the fight onto German soil in 1944, and even to end the war that year.

There was pride that the British First Airborne Division, and First Polish Parachute Brigade, were given the furthest target, and that they were to be carried in British aircraft. The 101st and 82nd American Airborne Divisions were briefed to take the two nearer targets.

The sheer scale of the operation can be judged by a few numbers. Twenty squadrons were to be involved with the airlift and they were supported by 27 squadrons of fighters and fighter bombers. Over 20,000 paratroops were to be dropped, and nearly 14,000 glider-borne men were also to be carried. In the follow-up, over 2,500 tonnes of supplies were eventually dropped. On the first day, the air armada took sixty-five minutes to pass overhead.

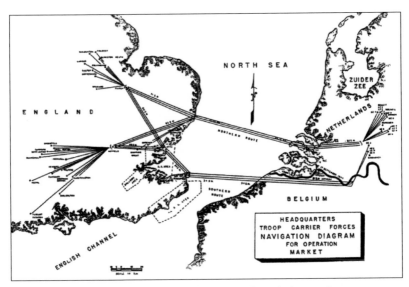

Routes for Market Garden. Fairford aircraft took the northern route.

W/C Lee's Stirling – all returned safely to England.

Rightly or wrongly, army and RAF briefings were held independently. There was little contact with the troops before take-off. The briefings were brisk and efficient, but not as detailed as they had been before D-Day. The intelligence briefing led us to believe that there would be little or no anti-aircraft resistance as the Arnhem area was garrisoned by troops of low morale.

It was difficult not to feel emotion as one came into contact with the men of the First Airborne Division. There were the hardened regulars – apparently taking the whole enterprise as almost routine and, at the other end of the scale, there were the unashamedly white-faced, lip-biting young troopers.

On the first day, 190 Squadron was detailed to carry pathfinder paratroops ahead of the main force. Their role was to secure the landing grounds and to clear them of obstacles, they also

Wing Commander Graeme Harrison puts Group Captain Allen Wheeler in the picture. First day of Market Garden.

2·00pm 18th September 1944.
Reproduced with the permission of the artist, Steven Warwick-Fleming.
A depiction of GHC's Stirling.

Lining up for Arnhem.

carried in Rebecca Eureka equipment to ease navigation into the landing area. On a lovely September afternoon, the twelve aircraft concerned flew in a loose formation of pairs. No briefing could have been more accurate; medium, low and high-level fighter cover was unobtrusive, but very effective, and there was nothing but the most modest flak opposition. All went well, the paratroops left the aircraft on time, all parachutes were seen to open, and the squadron climbed away to an uneventful flight home, with the astonishing sight of the air armada homing in towards the various landing areas.

The next day, 190 Squadron was briefed to tow Horsas. Before take-off the normal procedure for these operations was for the gliders to be packed in nose-to-tail on one side of the runway, while the Stirlings taxied on one after another; we had had so much practice of this that it was a smooth and slick operation. The tug lined up, and immediately the Horsa was towed in behind, the rope was attached and one of the ground crew signalled the tug slowly forward, the rear gunner in a Stirling was able to keep his pilot informed, and Tiny Shaw always did so, reporting when the nylon rope was taut. The final signal for take-off was given by a green light. Take-off was nearly always uneventful; the glider would be airborne in about 200 yards and helped to lift the tail of the tug, which made it possible to open the throttle fully rather earlier than usual. The take-off appeared long and cumbersome, and a slow climb away accentuated this sensation. Usually the Horsa dropped into the low-tow position at about 1,000 feet. This position below the tail of the tug gave the glider pilot the best possible visibility. There was a primitive intercommunication system between the two pilots, but it was seldom possible to exchange anything more than monosyllabic messages.

On the second day of Operation Market Garden, although not quite as quiet as the first, all went smoothly and again flying in loose formation, tug–glider combinations made their rendezvous on time, and then straggled out in an impressive stream. Take-off had been delayed because of fog over the fighter airfields in Belgium; this delay, one has subsequently learnt, was fortuitous since patrolling Messerschmidt 109's had needed to return to their bases to refuel. The occasional combination broke-up, usually when a tow-rope snapped. As we approached the landing zone a fair amount of light flak was in evidence, but there was an added anxiety with our aircraft. The starboard inner engine was rapidly losing oil pressure, and it would be touch-and-go whether we

YEAR 1944		AIRCRAFT		PILOT, OR 1ST PILOT	2ND PILOT, PUPIL OR PASSENGER	DUTY (Including Results and Remarks)
MONTH	DATE	Type	No.			
—	—	—	—	—	—	Totals Brought Forward
						SAS OPERATION S.E. PARIS
SEPT	5	STIRLING	939	SELF	CREW	24 CONTAINERS 4 PANNIERS
SEPT	9	STIRLING	431	SELF	CREW	AIR TEST
SEPT	16	STIRLING	918	SELF	CREW	AIR TEST
SEPT	16	STIRLING	431	SELF	CREW	AIR TEST
SEPT	17	STIRLING	431	SELF	CREW	OPERATION MARKET P.FF 15 P'TPS NR ARNHEM
SEPT	18	STIRLING	431	SELF	CREW	OPERATION MARKET II 16TH HORSA NR ARNHEM S.1 PEATHERED FLAK
SEPT	20	STIRLING	824	SELF	CREW	OPERATION MARKET RE-SUPPLY NR ARNHEM 24 CONTAINERS RE-SUPPLY
SEPT	23	STIRLING	824	SELF	CREW	OPERATION MARKET 24 CONTAINERS 4 PANNIER NR ARNHEM SOE OPERATION S OF ZUIDER ZEE
SEPT	30	STIRLING	962	SELF	CREW	OPERATION MARKET NO RECEPTION BAD WEATHER
				Summary for	SEPTEMBER	1944 1 STIRLING
				Unit	190 SQUADRON	
				Date	1·10·44	Types 3.
				Signature	E.H. Chesleton F/O	
				SUMMARY TUISINS		
				SUMMARY PARATROOPS		
				SIGND	O.C A FLIGHT	E.H.Chesleton F/O

Log book entries for Arnhem.

would make the last mile or two. All was well, and with a bellow of 'Goodbye and good luck' the glider cast-off and was seen by Tiny to circle and finally to settle heavily, but safely, amongst the rapidly accumulating force. The calm voice of Jack McCready came over the intercom, 'Skipper, you must feather the starboard inner immediately.' On three engines, the return journey was rather sluggish, followed by a very indifferent landing which used up every inch of the runway. This was greeted with derision by John Gilliard, my Flight Commander. It is awful to reflect that within twenty-four hours this splendid man had been killed.

190 Squadron had been remarkably lucky through the long summer of 1944, only losing three aircraft in this period, which included D-Day and the aftermath. With resupply at Arnhem, all this was about to change. The Germans had reacted to the airborne invasion with savage efficiency and by day three of the operation flak was horrendous, the most effective coming from a large number of quick firing self-propelled 88mm guns. Having been involved on the first two days, I was rested for the first day of resupply.

On this third day, Warrant Officer Stanley Coeshott and his crew were hit many times by flak and crashed with no survivors. John Gilliard, A-Flight's Commander, and my personal friend, had dropped his load of containers and panniers, when he was hit by flak near the tail. The two dispatchers were killed and probably also the rear gunner. Gilliard stayed at the controls until all the rest had bailed out, and was still there when the Stirling crashed out of control. Reginald Lawton, the navigator, joined the British troops on the ground, and eventually escaped across the Rhine after a series of hair-raising adventures. Frank Pascoe's aircraft was badly hit, and two of the crew injured, but he brought his Stirling safely home.

One of the problems over the Arnhem enterprise was the poor quality of the radio sets used by the troops on the ground. It was said that these were developed for use in the desert campaigns of North Africa. As a result of poor communication there was confusion about dropping zones, and there is little doubt that nearly 80% of the supplies dropped fell straight into enemy hands. Also, the dropping zones were fairly small, and there was considerable bunching of aircraft with a tendency for some to drop their loads too high. On the 20th of September, the fourth day of the operation, the Fairford squadrons were the last two scheduled for the Arnhem area. 190 Squadron with seventeen aircraft took-off at 1500 hours. The last few miles approaching the drop zone was an amazing sight. No doubt quite beautiful, if it wasn't so lethal. The flak bursts, some from 88s, some from Bofors-type quick-firing guns, punctuated the whole sky. It was almost impossible to retain the loose formation of pairs; I threw our Stirling into a violent corkscrew pattern and, although shrapnel could be heard hitting the fabric of the aircraft, we received no direct hits. Approaching the dropping zone at a height of 600 feet and a speed of about 150 knots, through lines of quick firing guns, was a stomach-turning experience. Happily, conscious memory seems to blur the details, though I still remember, to my shame, as Roderick Matheson's aircraft plummeted to the ground in a ball of fire, saying out loud, 'Thank God its not us!' Nightmares of this lived with me for years. As we dropped our load and went to climb away to starboard, there was such a gaggle of weaving Stirlings flying through a wall of flak that I decided to dive for the ground – and at full throttle. We screamed out of the area just above the trees; seldom has a Stirling travelled so fast. This we repeated on the last day, and came away virtually unscathed, but there was still worse to come.

No Skittles Tonight

The 21st of September was the fifth day of Operation Market Garden. I was again on the ground. Only 21 aircraft were available from the two squadrons at Fairford. The support fighters based in Belgium were fog bound and could not take off, thus exposing the resupply aircraft to German fighter opposition and an increased volume of flak.

I went to see the crews off just after mid-day; they would not be back for about four and a half hours. Some of us were due to play in a skittles match at the Royal Oak, a pub some three miles down the road, so I borrowed the squadron bicycle, an awful old bone shaker, and set-off to make final arrangements. The locals in the pub were well up-to-date over the events of the last few days, and were delighted that we planned to go ahead with skittles that evening.

Meanwhile, the 190 Squadron aircraft over Holland had run into even worse trouble than the day before. One was shot down before reaching the dropping zone; he was hit by flak and subsequently attacked by six ME 109s, three of the crew baled out before the aircraft broke up in midair. Wing Commander Harrison, who was leading the 190 detail, managed to drop his load but, as he turned for home, was shot down by prowling fighters; there were no survivors. Percy Siegert was attacked by two 109s, although suffering damage he dived to ground level whilst his rear gunner shot down one of his pursuers; he returned safely to Fairford. Sandy Anderson, A-Flight's Deputy Commander, was the next to go. They had been expecting an escort of American fighters; when they had dropped their load the rear gunner called out, 'There's our escort ... Christ, no – they're Jerrys!' They were badly shot up and were too low for anyone to bale out, Sandy skilfully managed to flop down on the River Maas. Unfortunately, the aircraft sank quickly and all but two were drowned.

Flying Officer Farren suffered in much the same way as the others. First he was hit by flak, and then he became easy meat for the fighters; three were killed, the survivors, some seriously wounded, eventually made their way to the Allied lines. John Hay was the next, he made a safe belly landing having suffered serious damage; the crew were all taken prisoner. Frank Pascoe suffered a similar fate to the others, with two engines on fire he crash landed on a ploughed field. The aircraft was ablaze from nose to tail, but, so skilful had been the landing, that eight members of the crew assembled as though it had been a routine practice; they were anxious that there was no sign of the captain, until he strolled calmly round from the other side of the aircraft. They were all back at Fairford within two days. Bob Herger had taken off rather later than the main detail, the flak was by then horrendous and, although they dropped their supplies, their Stirling was soon on fire; there were only two survivors. Two aircraft from 620 squadron were shot down, and two made forced landings elsewhere. Only three 190 Squadron Stirlings returned to base. It was not long before the news filtered through that the dropping zones were entirely in enemy hands, so the resupply mission had been doomed to failure, even before take-off. White-faced and trembling, I went to the nearest telephone and rang the Royal Oak, my message was simple, 'No skittles tonight!'

The Letter

On the 22nd of September, weather conditions ruled out any resupply for Arnhem, but it improved on the 23rd; the two squadrons at Fairford could only raise eighteen aircraft, 190 Squadron offered a mere seven. The situation on the ground at Arnhem was by now desperate, the guns of the Second Army could be heard, but this relieving force was still several miles away, and they were suffering serious losses and casualties in their efforts to breakthrough. Resupply was vital from the air, but communications had almost broken down, and dropping zones were likely to be in enemy hands. There was, nonetheless, not a thought of holding back, we had to try and get supplies through.

Earlier in the year, before D-Day, the adjutant of 190 Squadron had offered to hold last-minute letters to wives and families. I had taken him up on this offer and had written a long letter of totally sincere but no doubt rather cloying sentiment, to my dear wife K. I was only too happy to destroy this letter when I left 190 Squadron. I was detailed for the resupply mission on the 23rd September; I didn't see how I could possibly survive another venture into that cauldron of horror, so I felt I should write to my parents, and so I did. I wrote expressing my love and gratitude for everything that they had so unstintingly given to me as I grew up, and I particularly expressed my gratitude for my mother's silent support over the last few months. I gave this letter, with an unfortunately unclear instruction, to Percy Siegert (later Senior Air Officer in the RNZAF) asking him, if I failed to return, to post the letter. We were diverted due to bad weather on our return from Arnhem. So Percy posted it! Imagine my horror when I safely returned to discover that the letter was on the way home. I immediately rang my parents, the letter had arrived! My father, sensible and resourceful as he always was, had kept it from my mother until he knew I was safe. She then read it; I had expressed things which would otherwise never have been said, so I ceased cursing Percy Siegert.

Back to our resupply mission. Our detail was led by Wing Commander Lee, who commanded 620 squadron. All the fighter airfields were clear of fog and our 'little friends', as our own fighters were known, were present in abundance. No German aircraft left the ground, and the Allied fighters curbed flak activity as well. It was still an unpleasant experience, made even more distressing by the fact, as we discovered later, that the whole detail which followed Wing Commander Lee was nearly a mile off track. We all dropped in the same area, which was under enemy control. The reception was still unpleasant and, indeed, the Wing Commander was shot down. As we released our load and turned for home we dived to ground level, with Tiny Shaw blazing away at any opposition; he gave a whoop of delight, 'Skipper, I have just blown up a German petrol bowser!' Happily, all 190 aircraft returned safely and Wing Commander Lee and his crew had walked safely from their aircraft and were back in Fairford within a matter of days. This was the end of the ghastly Arnhem fiasco, which has since haunted me these sixty plus years.

It has never ceased to amaze me how the Dutch welcome those who were concerned with Market Garden, as though they really had brought them liberation. The true fact is that their attractive town was half destroyed, and all the Dutch in northern Holland suffered truly dreadful privations in the winter of 1944–45.

A Visit to the Opera

Two weeks, and two abortive SOE operations after Arnhem, an airborne venture in Yugoslavia was proposed. It was said at the time that this was one of Churchhill's schemes, designed to help Marshal Tito. 190 Squadron was detailed to tow Horsa gliders out to Italy, an enterprise which needed careful planning. We had to carry various spares, starter trollies, extra tow ropes, and all this involved the transport of ground crew.

Sixteen glider–tug combinations took off from Fairford. The object was to fly across France, which was by now almost totally liberated from the Germans, to refuel near Marseilles and fly on

Stirlings at Pomigliano with Vesuvius in the background.

to Rome. Each glider on this long haul carried two glider pilots, the concentration when being towed on such long distances was extremely tense, any careless movement could cause the breaking of the rope, although the ropes by this time were made of nylon, which had considerable elasticity. It was remarkable that fourteen combinations successfully completed the whole journey. The first leg to Istres, near Marseilles, was a record-breaking five and a half hour tow, travelling down through France via the Carcassonne Gate. The second, after an overnight stop, was the three and a half hour journey on to Rome, travelling mostly along the Mediterranean coast.

During our night stop at Istres we all made the most of our emergency rations – the glider pilots came into their own as they were more adept at handling primus stoves. We slept overnight in our aircraft. Having taken on fuel, we wallowed our way on to release our gliders at Cimpriano aerodrome near Rome, with shouts of good wishes down our primitive communication system. We had said goodbye to our glider pilots, but it was, in fact, not many days before they returned to England when the operation was cancelled. Perhaps the empty Horsa gliders had a future life as hen coops, or maybe as garden sheds. The destination of the tugs was further south, to Pomigliano, the airport for Naples. En-route, I decided that we should investigate Vesuvius, which was in full eruption. A decision I very soon regretted, the turbulence was alarming and we flew through the most unimaginably violent hail storm, we were thankful to seek the refuge of Pomigliano.

Naples had only recently been freed of the Germans; the city bore evidence of the bombing, shelling and fighting which only warfare brings. There were clearly desperate shortages, water being

the most obvious one, and it was impossible to avoid hordes of children begging in the streets. We were relatively comfortably housed aboard a troopship in the harbour. A visit to Pompeii was planned for the next day, but sadly there was no transport available; nonetheless, a free visit to the Opera was arranged for our final night in Naples. A full-scale performance of *Tosca* was showing at the Grand Opera House. This opera had started a week or two earlier, in defiance of the Germans, and now continued in celebration of their new-found freedom. 'Tosca' was clearly chosen for her magnificent voice, which filled the theatre, but she was a buxom lady and her final descent over the battlements was dramatic indeed. The next day, we flew back to England.

In the Dog House

There had been rumours for weeks that the two Fairford squadrons were on the move. A few days after returning from Naples, 190 and 620 Squadrons shipped lock, stock and barrel to Great Dunmow in Essex. This was a typical wartime station, which had originally been designed to take fighters; the particular snag where Stirlings were concerned, was the difficulty of taxiing on the perimeter track – there was only about eighteen inches clearance on either side of each wheel before descending into mud. Even the most graceful aircraft looks clumsy on the ground, and a Stirling more so than most. Steering was by means of the engines, and by the inadequate braking system. The brakes were pneumatic, fed by a small bottle of compressed air, this was replenished in flight through a compressor on the starboard inner engine or, when on the ground, externally from a larger bottle carried on a trolley.

A few days after arriving at Dunmow, we were detailed to carry a load of SAS paratroops in company with one other aircraft, the troops were detailed to capture an important bridge in eastern France. It was a dark night and taxiing halfway around the airfield was a nightmare. The compressed air bottle for the brakes was soon exhausted, long before we reached the runway; the reserve bottle on the trolley was sent for, and found to be empty. So much time had now been lost that the operation had to be aborted.

Next morning I was summoned to see the Air Officer commanding 38 Group at his headquarters some twenty miles away. This meant clean shoes and best uniform. When I arrived I marched into his office, gave him as smart a salute as I could manage, and prepared for the worst. It was not as bad as I feared, he said all the obvious things and I made the equally obvious apologies, to the point that I felt that I had come out of the interview as well as I could hope, and I could still hold up my head, but it didn't stop me getting stick in the Mess. I often wonder what happened to the ground crew responsible for keeping the trolley air bottle full.

Per Ardua ad Astra

A few days after the brake fiasco we were detailed for an SOE operation to Norway. The route would take us hundreds of miles across the North Sea – well beyond the range of any radar aids. Harry was a very good navigator, and on the rare occasions he had cause to use it, was a dab hand at astro. navigation. On this flight to Norway, he took a whole series of star shots, which confirmed our position as we progressed on our journey, and so excellent were his calculations – well supported by radio bearings from Jimmy – that our landfall just south-east of Oslo was only a quarter of a mile off the exact spot we hoped to reach on the coast. Indeed, the resistance group we were planning to contact heard our approach, and flashed the correct identification letter well in advance of our arrival. With a full fuel load, we could only carry 17 containers, these were safely dropped within ten minutes, and we started on the long slog home. As we had made our drop we had seen, some miles away, a vivid flash in the sky; we later discovered that this indicated the dying throes of a 620 aircraft which was shot down by fighters. Our fuel load had been over 2,300 gallons and about half-way back Jack McCready was anxious that we might be lower on fuel than was comfortable, so we diverted to Marston Moor in Yorkshire and put down there eight and a half hours after leaving base. We flew home to Dunmow the next day.

An End and a Beginning

Soon after the New Year of 1945 I was called in to see the Wing Commander, the new CO of 190 Squadron and a man I much respected. Wing Commander Bunker, who was tragically killed in a flying accident some two months later, surprised me by telling me that my first tour of operations was completed. This was a surprise because I believed that we had to carry out 30 operations; he went on to tell me that six months of operations was also a qualification. He had been asked to recommend two experienced crews to join a transport squadron which was being formed to blaze a new trail to the Far East. He was putting forward the names of Frank Pascoe and myself.

I suppose I could have declined his offer, but I think I realised it was right to change; K was five months pregnant and due in a few weeks to leave the WAAF, this move would relieve her of some anxiety. Since Arnhem, 190 Squadron had changed in character, not necessarily for the worse, but so many of my friends had gone that it was different, and I felt it might be sensible to move. Sadly, I had to say goodbye to Doug Smith, Tiny Shaw and Jimmy Knighton.

Doug had applied for a commission and, when this came through, he was remustered as a Transport Officer, by coincidence he was posted to St Mawgan – where my father was chaplain. He left the air force at the end of 1946 and returned to his earlier occupation of market gardening; he specialised in growing anemones. After his final retirement he moved to Guernsey and died there in 2006, his wife continues to live there.

190 Squadron Badge. Designed by Mrs Harrison and incorporating the double headed eagle from the Arnhem Coat of Arms.

Tiny Shaw remained at Dunmow as a supernumerary gunner, and very fortunate was any pilot to have him in his crew. When Tiny left the RAF he also returned to his earlier calling; that of a butcher.Indeed, now at his current age of 84, he is still working two days a week. Sadly, his wife died some years ago. Jimmy Knighton, on completion of the tour, was able to return happily to Canada with his wife Avril. He had met her at Dunmow and, indeed, on one occasion we smuggled her aboard a Stirling while we were doing an air test. He lives on the shores of Lake Ontario, sadly Avril died in 2007; they had had 62 happy years together.

Jack McCready and Harry Whiting, now a Warrant Officer, were able to join me on the venture into Transport Command. I had been more than fortunate with all these members in my crew, they were all utterly loyal, uncomplaining, unflappable and excellent contributors to a team effort.

Just before we left 190 Squadron, I attended the christenings of two young redheads, Tessa Harrison and John Gilliard, I am still in touch with them both.

LEONARD STANLEY

My father was posted as officiating chaplain at Moreton Vallance and Aston Down. Since neither of these stations was a full-time appointment, he also became vicar of the village of Leonard Stanley. A village that had a beautiful Norman church and an attractive, though cold and draughty, vicarage. It was easy to picture the comfort of living there a hundred years earlier. There had been stables, a superb walled garden and a tennis court. All had fallen into a state of disarray. My father was asked whether he would accept three German prisoners of war as gardeners, he needed little persuasion. Three men were dropped each morning and worked a full eight-hour day. The youngest was a defiant Nazi, but they were all good workers, and one was even a trained gardener. Within a matter of weeks the stables were converted to be a garage, the walled garden was restored, and planting was going on apace, even the tennis court was prepared for summer weather.

Transport Command

242 Squadron

With the war in Europe nearing its end, there was a greater concentration on activities looking to the East and planning further ahead, to building up an air transport system to India and beyond. Several squadrons were transferred to Transport Command to blaze the trail, including 242 Squadron initially equipped with Stirlings.

Summer 1945.

A generous fortnight's end-of-tour leave saw us finding our way, yet again, to Stoney Cross to join 242 Squadron. The three of us were joined by Ian Barkley, to be second pilot, and Ted Arnold to replace Jimmy Knighton as wireless operator, and we all prepared to launch into this new enterprise.

In Transport Command leave came in liberal chunks, after each trip to India we normally had five days, sometimes more. Just after Christmas of 1944, K had come out of the Air Force and had moved to Leonard Stanley, where my parents were by now fully established. I managed to get leave for the all-important day when Posy was born, April 18th, ('Posy' was my father's nickname for her, which has stuck all her life). It was long before, I am happy to say, the obligatory attendance of fathers at the bedside during a child's birth. I was strolling anxiously between the newly planted strawberries in the walled garden when Dr Mold appeared, he shook me by the hand and said, 'Congratulations, you are the father of a delightful, beautiful girl. Mother and daughter are doing well. I suggest you go and see them.' K's first public appearance, after this great event, was to join in the village VE day celebrations taking place round a bonfire. So Posy was, just, a wartime baby.

Yes, we have no Bananas

It was not until March that 242 Squadron was fitted out with Stirling Vs. This was a transport version of the Stirling; the main difference from earlier Marks, was the removal of the gun turret and a big loading door was cut out of the starboard side. The perspex nose was hinged so freight could be carried in the front of the aircraft, as well as in the rear. Some of the Mark Vs were kitted out to carry VIP passengers, but sadly none of these came the way of 242 Squadron.

After an initial training visit to North Africa, we launched out on our first so-called 'scheduled' flight. We took a load of spares to the depot in Karachi. The route took us to Castel Benito, the airport for Tripoli in North Africa; this was a long slog of about eight hours. Then the next leg, another long one, was to Lydda in Israel. Lydda to Shaibah, a ghastly place in the Iraqi desert, was the shortest leg. Then, finally, we moved on to Karachi, flying along the Gulf of Oman. We stayed two nights in Karachi before repeating the reverse route on the way back; we had left on March the 27th and returned on April 4th.

During the day at Stoney Cross, Customs Officials checked the incoming crews and passengers – they worked on a temporary basis coming out from Southampton. Since the flight took about eight hours, landings were usually after five in the afternoon and the Customs Officers had normally packed up and gone home. The ground crews were tipped off to warn us; thumbs up meant they had gone, thumbs down meant they were still there. If they had gone we filled in a Customs declaration form recording a few nominal articles, before wending our way. On this particular occasion we had just parked in the dispersal, having been given the thumbs up signal. I had filled in the Customs Form, declaring 200 cigarettes and a bottle of whisky, when, to my horror, I saw a sleek black car draw up with a very senior Customs Officer aboard. 'Right,' he said, 'All the crew can go except the captain.' I then unloaded all my treasures, carpets, towels, shoes, cigarettes, bananas and more besides, because everything was in short supply. The Customs Officer said, 'I am really out for a drive with my family, my six-year-old son has never seen a Stirling before, nor, of course, as he ever seen a banana.' Rapidly taking the hint, I broke off half a dozen from my large bunch, handed them over with some cheerful remark. Smiles all round, and the officer drove off with a cheerful wave.

A VE Day Tragedy

Quite out of the blue, we were given a totally different transport task. We were detailed to carry a load, about 50 I seem to remember, of drop tanks to an RAF station at Banff in Scotland. There was a Mosquito Squadron based there; the principal role of the squadron was to attack German shipping off the Norwegian coast. To give them a longer range, Mosquitoes were fitted with plastic tanks, which held enough fuel for a few extra hours flying time. This fuel was used first and then the tanks were discarded, hence the name 'drop tanks'. We arrived at Banff with our load during the afternoon of May 7th 1945, the day it was announced that the 8th would officially see the end of the war in Europe. The ghastly tragedy was that the day before, during the very last raid of the war, two Mosquitoes had been lost in an attack on a German convoy. As guests in a strange mess we were made very welcome to the monumental party that developed; but I couldn't get those two crews out of my mind.

Madras

It was a particular pleasure to have another officer in the crew. With 190 Squadron it hadn't really mattered, since we often went out together as a crew away from the actual RAF station and, anyway, I had many friends living in the mess. Out on the route with 242 Squadron, Ian Barkley and I often shared quarters together and at least we had each other's company in the mess.

Ian was a Wykehamist, it has to be said an unlikely one, but we did have much in common and became firm friends. It was an amazing coincidence that he turned up at Brasenose a year after I had been at Oxford, or did he in some way contrive it? During 1945 and much of 1946, we shared each other's company. It was a joy to have a second pilot, although I have to say I nearly always did the take-offs and landings and, needless to say, the automatic pilot took the tedium of flying from A to B; that is to say when it was working. About our third trip was to Madras. The RAF mess there was in a fine building from the early colonial days, which stood in a large handsome garden. The sleeping quarters, comfortably equipped, were in wooden chalets dotted

Ian Barkley

about the garden. Ian and I stayed there two nights, on the first, we went to change for dinner and set out along the tree-lined path back to the mess about a quarter of a mile away. We had left our chalet by some hundred yards when, in the dim half-light, we both saw an enormous king cobra gently coiled and swaying as though he was about to strike. Ian and I said nothing, but shot back to our chalet at record-breaking speed. We ventured forth with much trepidation, some ten minutes later, all was well; our friend had gone.

The next day we went down into the city of Madras. There was a considerable fracas developing in the main square, which we, out of curiosity, went to investigate. Suddenly, we became the centre of attention. It turned out that some African troops, presumably in transit, were arguing over the cost of some rickshaws they had hired. The Africans, and a growing tide of Indians, turned for arbitration to the two young English officers that had appeared on the scene. There was no backing off, both sides expected us to mete out proper justice. Fortunately a van load of riot police appeared on the scene at this tricky moment and we happily made ourselves scarce.

In Praise of Sikhs

The next trip was to Calcutta, my sister lived there, her husband being in the Indian Navy, and I had advised her that sometime in the near future I would pay her a visit. We were delivering some freight to Calcutta and landed at the airport, which was known as 'Dum Dum'. We were due to stay there about 36 hours; all the crew were put up in special lodging houses and I went to see exactly where they were, so I would be able to find them. I then called a taxi and travelled all the way across Calcutta to the attractive suburb where my sister lived; this was in great contrast to the village of Dum Dum near the airport, which was out of bounds to all British servicemen. The situation in India at this time was difficult for the British, because it was just before partition and every Indian wanted to see the back of us. However, it was lovely where my sister lived; I arrived just in time for dinner, and we sat up late, chatting about this and that. Before I went to bed, Margaret said to me, 'Just throw your clothes on the floor and they will be washed and ready for you to wear in the morning.' I could hardly believe it. I stayed most of the next day and Margaret showed me the local sights, I planned to leave her about teatime. However, she persuaded me to stay on and have dinner with her, saying that I could easily get a taxi back to the airport. We were due to take-off at midnight. About eight o'clock, we rang for a taxi; nearly all the taxis in Calcutta were operated by Sikhs and the one which came was no exception. A tall, handsome, bearded man was the driver, his assistant, who was much younger, was sitting in the passenger seat, but, like the driver, was well armed. I asked the driver to take me to the airport, he politely, but emphatically, refused. I told him that it was vital that I should make the journey across Calcutta. But he simply said that it was dangerous to pass through the village of Dum Dum in the dark. I again said that I had to get to the aerodrome, so he offered me a special price; he said that he would do the journey for 30 rupees – this was, I suppose, double what you would have to pay on the meter. My sister was furious, but I simply had to accept. We crossed through Calcutta and through the village of Dum Dum without any problem, but then I had to find the lodgings where I would find my crew, this proved to be much more difficult than I expected – in the dark I couldn't recognise any buildings. We drove out of one road, down the next, and, I suppose, desperately searching it must have been nearly half an hour before I suddenly spotted a landmark which I recognised. I asked the driver to pull up. This was the right spot. I climbed out and was ready to pay considerably more than the agreed price, because we had been so long on the journey; I noticed that his meter reading was 33 rupees. He refused to take any extra, and when I said, 'At least let me pay what is on the meter. He said, 'No Sahib, we agreed 30 chips and 30 chips it is!'

A sad sequel to this story, is that my sister Margaret, about six weeks after my visit, contracted polio. She was in an iron lung for some weeks, and then she reclined in a Calcutta hospital until, fortunately, the Navy managed to find her a place on a hospital ship going home to England. She arrived in Southampton and was taken from there to the Naval Hospital in Portsmouth, where she stayed for sometime before going to my parents house in Gloucestershire. She arrived there towards the end of October and, as she was being carried on a stretcher upstairs, she said, 'I will be downstairs for Christmas,' and so she was. She never made a full recovery and was always very much disabled, but still she brought up a family, and lived as normal a life as possible until she died at the age of 87. A real example of guts and determination.

THE MAJOR AND THE CARPET

Sometimes when we returned from India, we landed at Lyneham, there were much better facilities here for passengers than at our home bases, and there was a full-time Customs Service. The crews had to go through Customs alongside the passengers. The service was usually quick and sympathetic; nearly all our passengers were military personnel, returning home from overseas postings, usually after several years and, in many cases, from the battle areas of Burma.

On one such occasion there was, immediately ahead of me in the queue for Customs, a Royal Artillery Major – not actually from my aircraft. He had, on a trolley beside him, a fairly large, rolled-up carpet stitched neatly in a hessian covering. I had a similar bundle, though not quite so large, mine was a *Bambi* rug for my daughter Posy's nursery. The major, who I discovered had spent over two years in Burma, was instructed to undo his bundle. He protested on the grounds that it would be so difficult to carry it once it was undone, and he produced a receipt from a well-known Karachi carpet merchant, this was a standard procedure, but the official persisted and the poor Major had no choice but to cut his carpet free. There it was, an ordinary carpet, but wrapped inside it was an exquisite silk Persian rug, of considerable antiquity. He then disappeared to some nether region and my goods, carpet and all, went through on the nod.

By the merest chance, some half an hour later, I bumped into my Major friend about to leave the building. I had to ask him how he had fared. 'I suppose,' he said, 'I have been quite lucky. I have had to pay £300 duty on my rug, I imagine they let me keep it because I did not actually admit to any deceit, but it was touch and go whether or not I should be allowed to take it away. What I would really like to know, is who it was who split on me, because it was quite clear that the Customs Officer knew the rug was hidden inside the carpet.' We then went our separate ways.

TRAGEDY AT PALAM

Our last major trip to India in the dear old Stirling saw us again heading to Calcutta. This time, we took a load of freight out, and it was planned that we should bring passengers back. One of the features of these journeys was that not only did the crews go through Customs with passengers, but we often had meals with them as well. On our way out we landed at Palam, the airport for Delhi, and we coincided with a Liberator planeload of passengers heading home; there were twenty-five of them, all nurses, who had served about two years in Burma. We had breakfast at a long table with them and charming and interesting they were.

They took off immediately ahead of us and, as their Liberator climbed away from the end of the runway to head west, we followed to turn for our easterly journey. As we were climbing away, some five minutes later, Palam control called us, asking us to turn about to see if we could see anything of the Liberator. As we turned, in the distance was a horrible spiral of black smoke which, once seen, could only mean one thing. We raced back, diving as we went, and there, about fifteen miles west of Palam, was the blazing Liberator in the middle of a paddy field. There was thick black smoke and angry red flames engulfing the aircraft from end to end. Nothing, we believed, could survive in that inferno. We reported back to Palam with deep despair. Their advice was for us to resume our journey, and they told us several fire trucks were on the way to the Liberator. The usual cheerful chat we had over the intercom was totally muted; there was nothing to say.

Three days later, on our return journey, we naturally inquired about the plane load of nurses. The news overjoyed us. All but three on the Liberator survived. What had happened was that, shortly after take-off, one of the engines had caught fire, the pilot had been unable to put the fire out and so had no choice but to make an immediate crash landing. He put the aircraft down with great skill in a paddy field, unfortunately, the impact of the crash landing smashed the main spar, part of which crushed three of the passengers – it was believed they were killed instantly; the rest escaped without any injury, an almost unbelievable achievement, but still a tragedy.

Over to the York

In December of 1945 242 Squadron was moved to Merryfield, yet another wartime station of dispersed nissen huts. None of us understood why the move was made, life was just as inconvenient as it had been at Stoney Cross. A few months before, Douglas Bader had come home from a prisoner of war camp, he was now a Group Captain and something of a national hero. His first major command, back in 1940, had been 242 Squadron – it was then a Canadian squadron which had suffered heavy losses, and morale was low. Douglas Bader had not only restored their reputation and pride, but made it one of the most successful squadrons in the Battle of Britain. That it had now become a transport Squadron was a matter for hardly concealed disgust on his part, nonetheless, he accepted an invitation to a grand Ball, to celebrate his survival and the end of the war.

Harry Whiting, Jack McReady, Ted Arnold, Ian Barkley, George Chesterton.

K was able to leave Posy with my mother, and we found a room at a local hostelry. At the Ball, Douglas Bader stumped round the floor on his tin legs with K, whose company he found to his liking. Years later, when I met him again, he laughed, remembering the evening with much pleasure, but the idea of 242 Squadron being a Transport Squadron still rankled.

It was now that the Stirling was superseded by the Avro York. This was a transport version of the Lancaster, powered by the same beautiful Merlin engines. It was intended to be the British answer to the Dakota, something which it never achieved, but for all that it was a fine aeroplane and a joy to fly. One of the unusual features of the York was that the throttles were in the roof above the pilot's head. The passenger accommodation was a vast improvement on the Stirling. The RAF fleet of Yorks not only did valiant service on the transport routes but, in 1948, valuable work was done

The Avro York

on the Berlin air-lift; indeed, without the York the British effort would have been minimal. It was sad to say goodbye to the dear old Stirlings, and the regrettable thing is that they were flown up to Yorkshire to be broken up. A few were bought by a Belgian airline, but they were soon out of service and there is not a single survivor of the 2,000 made anywhere in the world.

A Blind Date

Our furthest journey was to Ceylon, where we were to take out a load of freight. On the long slog eastwards across North Africa there came the news of the second atomic bomb on Nagasaki, and the subsequent immediate surrender of the Japanese. For us, although it was exciting news, it was a slightly damp squib since we were in no position to celebrate; we pressed on for Ceylon which we reached two days later.

The RAF station in Ceylon was Ratmalana; some months earlier, a WAAF friend of K's was posted there. VJ parties were in full swing when we arrived and we were told that we wouldn't start our return journey for three days, since there would then be some passengers for us to bring home. I decided to get in touch with K's friend Mary Ellis. I made contact by phone and she agreed that we should meet the next evening at six o'clock. At her suggestion we were to meet in the Gall Face Hotel in the middle of Colombo. The hotel was a vast, colonial-style building with enormous Palladian pillars; it is still there, although it has lost some of its former glory. Mary told me that she would be easy to recognise since she had bright red hair.

I arrived at the hotel in good time, and simply could not believe the number of attractive girls there were in Colombo, and a lot of them seemed to be redheads. WRNS, in their smart white uniforms, far outnumbered the WAAFS and the ATS, who were all in khaki. At last, and I believe blind dates, like brides, are expected to be late, Mary arrived. Although I had half climbed out of my seat several times, there was now no doubt – her hair wasn't quite carroty, but it was very red, combined with a slim figure, and her smart khaki uniform, she made a blind date to be proud of.

We went to an outdoor cinema together, and agreed to meet the next day. She had planned that we would go round a whole host of backstreet dealers in saphires. Her idea, and rather a jolly one, was that I should buy enough saphires to have an eternity ring made up for K. It turned out as a partial success, but my finances had not made it possible to buy really good matching stones. Mary was on duty next day, so I didn't see her again, but I am still in touch with her; she lives in Sidmouth.

THE SOUTH AFRICAN GENERAL

Sometimes the Iraqi desert is beset by line squalls, which include violent thunderstorms; from a flying point of view these result in spectacular and alarming turbulence. Modern aircraft simply climb above such storms, but in the 1940s no oxygen was carried, so the maximum practical height was 10,000 feet. On our way home in mid-1945 with a planeload of servicemen returning from the Far East, somewhat unexpectedly, we had amongst them a South African General. We left Shaibah on the leg of the journey to Lydda, it was just after dark and very shortly we ran into violent thunder and lightning, with the accompanying turbulence. Ahead

of us the conditions appeared to be very much worse and I decided there was some risk of structural damage, so the sensible course was to return to Shaibah and try again in the morning, when the storms had abated.

I went back to tell our passengers of my decision, half of them, poor things, had sick bags in front of them, and several were clearly very frightened as the aircraft was thrown violently about the sky. I communicated my message with considerable difficulty, since it was almost impossible to retain any sort of balance. I told the general, who immediately objected, saying that he had a connection to make in London for a flight to South Africa. He said, 'I order you to continue to Lydda'. Needless to say, I was having none of this, and told him that my decision was final, and was made principally for the safety of everyone in the aircraft. I returned to my position on the flight deck, and was astonished a few minutes later to find the general alongside me. 'I order you to resume our journey to Lydda'. As politely as possible I reminded him that I was captain of the aircraft. 'If you don't obey my orders, I will have you court-martialled', he bellowed at me. 'Sir,' I replied, 'If you don't return to your seat immediately, I shall place you under arrest.' An apoplectic general disappeared to his seat.

In due course we all spent the night safely back in Shaibah. Naturally, I reported the unhappy incident with the General to the Wing Commander in charge of flying, he merely said, 'My only regret is that you didn't actually put the general under arrest.' Fortunately there was another York on the way home, leaving about the same time as we were. By mutual agreement the South African General changed to this aircraft. Needless to say, I never heard another word about this episode.

A Side of Beef

In transport command the regular crew in four engined aircraft numbered five; the first pilot and captain, a second pilot, a navigator, the wireless operator and a flight engineer. When passengers were carried an extra member joined the crew, his title was the rather pretentious 'Air Quartermaster', a grand name for a steward. The likelihood of having the same quartermaster on different flights was fairly remote.

In June 1946, we were detailed to pick up some radar operators from the Azores. This was a long old slog, nearly eight hours and, once again, Harry Whiting proved his skill as a navigator; we homed straight in on Lagens, the main airport for the islands. We only stayed one night and there was little opportunity for much shopping, but I remember buying some pink bath towels for my mother, something she had not seen new for six years.

Our return flight started at dusk. Our plane load of passengers was aboard, all the crew were at their stations, but no sign of the air quartermaster. I was about to start the engines and leave without him when there was a flurry of excitement and across the tarmac came the missing quartermaster, followed by two porters. It was not immediately evident what the porters were carrying, whatever it was they were pursued by hordes of flies. As they drew closer it became clear they were carrying a side of beef. It was difficult, despite all the breaches of discipline, to keep a straight face and when the quartermaster was told that his precious purchase must be left on the tarmac, the poor man almost broke down in tears. Then I had to impose a bit of discipline, 'Not only have you made an illegal purchase, but you have reported for duty two hours late, totally ignored your paperwork and have neglected your charges; I have no choice but to put you under open arrest. Now please make sure you make the comfort and well being of the passengers you're only concern for the next eight hours.

I have often wondered what happened to the side of beef. After an uneventful flight home I relented, and told the quartermaster that I would release him from arrest but appealed to him never to fly with us again.

Demob and Cricket

A well planned system was devised for the release of servicemen into civilian life. After the 1914–18 war, members of the services flooded the labour market, causing considerable distress. Under the new scheme, every soldier, sailor and airman was given a demobilisation number related to his length of service. My number was 35. Once the war was over the phased release began. It was possible, if an individual had cause for quick release, to appeal, and he would probably be able to leave earlier. My release was scheduled for February 1946, but the planners, in their wisdom, found they were running short of experienced, four engined aircraft pilots. Therefore, with no option, my service was extended by six months. Nothing could have suited me better, I was due to start at Oxford in October, so this extra six months in the RAF was ideal.

At the end of April, 242 Squadron moved again, this time to Oakington near Cambridge, the first permanent RAF station I had experienced. K and I had been married all but three years, the move to Oakington, in a more relaxed peacetime atmosphere, gave us an opportunity to set-up house for the first time. We shared part of a large, handsome Georgian building in the village of Fenstanton with Clive Halse, my flight commander, and his Belgian wife Penny; a very happy arrangement. Peacetime activities became important again. I had little hesitation in putting my name forward when cricketers were asked for. A series of trial games were held at Vine Lane, Uxbridge and, to my astonishment, I made a meteoric advance up the cricket ladder finding myself picked to play for the RAF. Apart from what was called monthly training, which took an hour or so of flying, cricket seemed to take priority. Training and practice for the inter-service matches at Lord's were regarded as more important than trips to the Far East. My crew didn't object too much, since they had longish periods of extended leave.

Lord's

Having been selected to play cricket for the Royal Air Force in the inter-service matches at Lord's, my flying programme was very much reduced, indeed, it turned out that our trip to the Azores was the last major journey we made as a crew.

All the service elevens were reasonably strong, each side had at least three former professional cricketers upon whom to call. Our first match was against the army, towards the end of July. Remembering my previous visit to Lord's for an FFI nearly four and a half years earlier, the ground looked in wonderful condition, and a great contrast to the barrage balloons and barbed wire I remembered. It was astonishing, the public turned out in considerable numbers to watch these matches, an indication of how much we had all been starved of any entertainment through nearly six years of war.

At Lord's.

The layout at Lord's, to this day as well as in 1946, is somewhat unusual in that the dressing rooms for the opposing teams are sited at opposite ends of the building and on the first floor. Therefore, if a wicket fell, and you were next to bat, you had to go downstairs, through the Long Room and out onto the hallowed turf. When my turn to bat came and I started on my way down, what I didn't realise is that the stairs lead further down to a basement, where the lavatories are sited and, of course, this is where I went. I was in the ghastly state that I didn't know where to go. I am sure I was not the first person to do this, and I'm equally sure that there will be many more in the future. When I eventually found my way to the wicket the bowling seemed much more terrifying, particularly as I confronted a muscular red-head by the name of Dick Pollard, who had opened the bowling for Lancashire and England in 1939. Fortunately, it worked out well and I made a few runs; 30 not out! It was difficult to achieve a result in a two-day match at the best of times, but rain also interrupted play and, for a time, the light was so bad that Dick Pollard sportingly bowled at half pace; a draw became inevitable. The match against the Navy followed a similar pattern, although the weather played only a minor part, but a dour struggle followed with a draw being the only possible result. For all that, each of these matches was played in a festival spirit and on each occasion was enlivened by a Royal Air Force band.

BERLIN AND CRICKET

With the inter-service cricket matches at Lord's behind us, I was expecting to be back on the route to India; not so, I was invited to take part in a RAF cricket tour to play against British sides in Germany. My delightful squadron commander, Billy Wicht, a Swiss who had joined the Royal Air Force in the thirties, saw no objection and, indeed, encouraged me to go. The intention was to play four matches against Army and RAF teams during the last 10 days of August. The team was flown to Germany in three Ansons, something of a squash. The climax of the tour was to be a visit to Berlin for a two day match on the ground developed just outside the Olympic Stadium. After the first three matches, a cheerful and noisy bus load of cricketers was stunned into silence by the horrors of the approach into Berlin. Hardly a building was standing and mere mounds of bricks and mortar marked the former sites of houses, many of these piles had a simple wooden cross standing above the rubble. It was hard to believe that such damage could be achieved by bombing and on this the western side of the city, it undoubtedly was. Berlin was still an open city, and we were free to roam at will. Very informal tours of Hitler's bunker were conducted by cheerful Russian soldiers; Eva Braun's furniture was still in situ. I even helped myself to some pieces of gold mosaic, with an idea of making them into earrings for K, I am happy to say, she thought this was in very poor taste. Overawed, as one could not fail to be by such wholesale destruction, it was a pleasure to come to the Olympic Stadium, which miraculously was not seriously damaged. Our cricket match was won comfortably enough and we flew back to Northolt with memories of the horrors of Berlin far exceeding any nightmares we could have imagined.

PLEASE DISPLAY THIS ON YOUR NOTICE BOARD!

CRICKET

BRITISH TROOPS BERLIN

v

THE ADASTRIAN CRICKET CLUB

**FRIDAY AND SATURDAY
30 AND 31 AUGUST 1946**

ON

THE GARRISON GROUND

OPPOSITE

THE OLYMPIC SPORTS CLUB

PLAY COMMENCING EACH DAY AT 11.30 HOURS

ADMISSION FREE

Cricket was still not over. During the summer there had been an Inter Command Knockout Competition leading towards a final at the Oval. Transport Command had disposed of Fighter and Training Commands on the way, and early in September we played out an inconclusive final against Coastal Command. We were now into September, and my time to become a civilian would shortly be due. I put in occasional appearances at Oakington. It seemed to be a tradition that young retiring officers should be allotted a last day's duty as Orderly Officer. This meant inspecting the lavatories, paying a visit to the airman's mess, going to the guardroom lock up – there were no residents during my duty, mounting the guard and various other mundane tasks. I had to do a monthly flying test, both at day and night, rather pointless, since it was obvious that I would not be going out on the route again, but at least I felt part of the squadron scene.

There were fairly frequent farewell parties, as one by one demob time came to sundry members of the squadron. I continued to live happily with the Halses at Fenstanton. On one or two occasions, K and I made expeditions to London while the Halses looked after Posy. One such visit stands out in my memory. We went to join a party in London to go to the theatre. There was a generally festive atmosphere. After the interval half way through the play, I gave my relatively new zip fly a reassuring tug – there was, I suppose, half an inch of slack to be taken up. To my complete horror, I zipped myself into the dress of an attractive young woman, who was ahead of me in the press to return to our seats. It was a beautiful red satin dress, brought out no doubt for some special celebration. We were like Siamese twins, and the more I struggled to release her, the more firmly we were joined. An usherette eventually frog marched us to the manager's office. The manager tried to release us; K found us in the office and tried to rescue the situation, it was eventually agreed a pair of scissors was the only answer. The manager carried out the operation, which inevitably left a star shaped hole in the back of the poor girl's dress. She was charming and thankful to be free, I never saw her again.

There was a remarkable scheme devised, whereby every serviceman, and I suppose servicewoman, attended a despatch centre. Here there was the opportunity to choose two complete changes of civilian clothing. It was a slick and well-organised procedure; on arrival release documents were studied, and then a large cardboard box was handed over. For many this would be the immediate receptacle for the uniform they were wearing. But for the majority the new civilian clothes could be carried away safely in the box. The choices of clothes and the quality were extremely variable. I possessed no civilian suit, so this was a must. There were four possibilities from which to choose, two were horrendous, one was funereal and one was an acceptable tweed. There were shirts, socks, ties, and even an overcoat. Each individual's entitlement also included headgear; I chose a Tyrolean trilby which I am sure I never wore, and so I stepped out into civilian life.